*Equipping and Empowering
Everyday Believers to Live
in the Realm of the Spirit*

Æk.tɪ.veɪt: to awaken, trigger or set in motion

GABBY CONLON

ACTIVATE

Equipping and Empowering Everyday Believers to Live in the Realm of the Spirit

Copyright © 2024 Gabby Conlon

Request for information should be addressed to: gabbyconlon@gmail.com

ISBN: 978-0-6486380-0-1

All rights reserved. No part of this publication may be reproduced, stored in a retrieval system, or transmitted in any form or by any means – electronic, mechanical, photocopy, recording or any other – except for brief quotations in printed reviews, without the prior permission of the author.

 A catalogue record for this book is available from the National Library of Australia

For Worldwide Distribution

All Scripture quotations are indicated.

Scripture quotations marked (NLT) are taken from the Holy Bible, New Living Translation, copyright ©1996, 2004, 2015 by Tyndale House Foundation. Used by permission of Tyndale House Publishers, Carol Stream, Illinois 60188. All rights reserved.

Scripture quotations marked (ESV) are from The ESV® Bible (The Holy Bible, English Standard Version®), copyright © 2001 by Crossway, a publishing ministry of Good News Publishers. Used by permission. All rights reserved.

Scripture quotations marked (BSB) are taken from The Holy Bible, Berean Study Bible, BSB Copyright © 2016, 2020, 2022 by Bible Hub. Used by Permission. All Rights Reserved Worldwide.

Scripture quotations marked (TPT) are from The Passion Translation®. Copyright © 2017, 2018, 2020 by Passion & Fire Ministries, Inc. Used by permission. All rights reserved. ThePassionTranslation.com.

Scripture quotations marked (NKJV) are taken from the New King James Version®. Copyright © 1982 by Thomas Nelson. Used by permission. All rights reserved.

Scripture quotations marked (AMP) are taken from the Amplified Bible, Copyright © 2015 by The Lockman Foundation. Used by permission.

Scripture quotations marked (NIV) are taken from the Holy Bible, New International Version®, NIV®. Copyright © 1973, 1978, 1984, 2011 by Biblica, Inc.™ Used by permission of Zondervan. All rights reserved worldwide. www.zondervan.com

The "NIV" and "New International Version" are trademarks registered in the United States Patent and Trademark Office by Biblica, Inc.™

Editor: Monika Zanardo
Illustrator: Bonnie Molesworth
Cover Design: #optimalgraphics
Produced for the Author by Eric at exlibris.com.au

Activate is for all who long for the 'more' of heaven. To read this book is to sit with the One so worthy, and that's exactly what Gabby and Jesus had in mind. As you dive into its pages, you will be beautifully undone and then gloriously rebuilt to live a life of awe and wonder.

I have known Gabby for many years, and few people I know love Jesus like her, with such passion and humility. To know her is to know Him. I am thankful for this book and the wisdom and revelation Gabby brings to the table. May it compel you to lean in closer to the heartbeat of heaven and lead you into encounters you never dreamed possible.

~ **Fiona Griffiths, Author, Speaker, Writing Coach**
thehappyscribe.com.au

I have known and ministered with Gabby for over 25 years and I'm so excited to see this book take shape. *Activate* is one of the most helpful and timely books I've read. In my years of ministry and church leadership I've yet to find a resource that is so practical in teaching people how to connect with the Spirit of God in their lives and to be led by Him. The Bible says that in the last days there will be many people 'having the appearance of godliness but denying its power'. (2 Timothy 3:5)

Through her practical activations, teaching, personal stories and examples, Gabby takes you on a journey of connecting with the tangible presence of God as He always intended. Whether as an individual or used in a group, it will help you move from simply knowing about God to becoming aware of His presence and His leading in every area of your life. This book puts the adventure back into loving and following Jesus and shows us that what we often call 'radical' is actually how God always intended us to live.

~ **Matthew Doty, Lead Pastor, Melbourne Lights Church**

Gabby has unique insight into her friend, the Holy Spirit. Her passion for Holy Spirit will stir your hunger to know Him more! Gabby's new book *Activate* will connect you in with Holy Spirit and help you on your journey to move in supernatural gifts, just as she has helped many students here at the School of Faith. I commend both Gabby and her new book to anyone looking to develop more intimacy with Him.

~ **Tristan Conway, Director School of Faith**

Having read *Activate* by my friend and kingdom colleague Gabby Conlon, I said to myself: this is such a 'now' book. Having known Gabby and her husband David for the last 8 years and ministered with them for the last 5, I can honestly say that each chapter, containing a brief teaching followed by a practical series of activations, is an expression and extension of how Gabby lives daily. Gabby lives for the audience of 'one'; Jesus. Gabby is a gifted prophet, practical teacher and releaser of the person, presence and power of the Holy Spirit. I highly endorse *Activate* and know it will release each reader to be 'positioned' for more of the Holy Spirit.

~ Paul Zanardo, Pastor, Author of *Finding Issachar: Wisdom and Know-How in Uncertain Times*

Activate is an invaluable tool for every Christian as a powerful way to enter into encounter in our times of abiding in the secret place. I believe it will also be valuable as a tool for people to meet and start a relationship with Jesus. I enjoyed doing a couple of the activations as I read through the book and they led to deep revelations and encounters with Father God, Jesus and Holy Spirit. I can't wait to do the rest! Knowing Gabby personally through co-labouring in the Kingdom together on team at Melbourne Lights Church, I can attest to her integrity and life passion to see lives transformed by Holy Spirit encounters. It is always so exciting to hear the powerful testimonies that result from these activations.

~ Monika Zanardo, Melbourne Lights Church Leadership Team, Author of *{Re}Finding Joy: when you have lost some joy [or never knew where to find it]*

Acknowledgments

To Jesus. I am forever thankful for your relentless, reckless, unconditional love that pursued me all those years ago and saved a 'wretch like me'. I will always be overwhelmed by your goodness and love towards me. Thank you for not only saving me but for healing me and setting me free. I am only where I am because of you. I am in awe that you would choose to reveal yourself and the realm of the spirit to me! That you would entrust me with this gift blows my mind! Thank you, Holy Spirit, for being my best friend and teacher. Writing this book was your idea and I am humbled that you invited me to partner with you in it.

To my amazing husband David and four incredible kids – Jessica, Bethany, Jordan and Amy. You are literally the wind beneath my wings! Thank you for cheering me on – always. I am forever thankful for the gifts each of you are to my life. Your encouragement and love feed my soul. I love each of you beyond words.

To my parents – Jim and Henryka. Thank you for your belief in me and my ability to one day write a book! You have always known it was something I wanted to do, even as a child. I am who I am and where I am because of your consistent love, support, encouragement, and prayers for me. I love you both.

To Monika Zanardo. How can I thank you enough? I had a dream to write a book but had no idea what to do once I had written it! Monika, you have blessed me beyond measure. Your expertise in all things related to publishing a book have made a dream into a reality. Thank you for your hours of proof-reading, editing, and formatting, not to mention your wisdom and knowledge around the 'how-tos' of writing and publishing. Your input was invaluable. You are a true gift.

To the Pastors team at my home church, Melbourne Lights Church. I love that I get to run on team with a bunch of crazy Jesus lovers! Your wisdom, authenticity and friendship have helped shape me. Your faith in me over the years, has empowered me to step into the call of God for my life. Thank you for championing me.

To the School of Faith Family. You were my guinea pigs! It was here that I got to write and test out all these activations first. Thank you to our

Director at SOF, Tristan Conway, who employed me in great faith to come on team in the early days of School, as the *Activations Pastor*. What a God set-up! Seeing people all over the world encounter Father, Son and Holy Spirit so profoundly through these simple activations not only surprised me but brought so much joy to my heart. It was the springboard for writing this very book.

To some special friends. Gabriel Lee and Megan Edwards, I am so very, very thankful for your love and support. You both encouraged me, spurred me on and kept me accountable over the last year, relentlessly checking in on my progress. Megan, you gave me the most direct prophetic word about writing this book when you had no idea it was even in process. It was the Holy Spirit kick up the butt that I needed!

Contents

Acknowledgments v
Introduction xi

CHAPTER 1
Positioned for Presence 1
   ACTIVATE 2
   1. Come as a Child – What's the Game? 2
   2. Heaven's Waterfall 4
   3. Road Trip with Jesus! 5
   4. Picnic with Jesus 6
   5. The Secret Garden 7

CHAPTER 2
Positioned for More 11
   ACTIVATE 13
   1. Dad's Toolbox 13
   2. Where in the World? 14
   3. Let's Go Fruit Picking 16
   4. Treasure Box 17
   5. Cave of Wonders 18

CHAPTER 3
Positioned in Love 21
   ACTIVATE 23
   1. Invitation to go on a Date 23
   2. The Banquet Table 24
   3. God's Glory Box 26
   4. May We Never Lose the Wonder 28
   5. Wrap Around Love 29

CHAPTER 4
Positioned to See   31

ACTIVATE   33
1. Look to See!   33
2. Street Signs   35
3. Revelation of Jesus – Look at His Face!   36
4. The Banner   38
5. Royal Coronation   39

CHAPTER 5
Positioned to Discern   43

ACTIVATE   45
1. Discerning the Angelic   45
2. Discerning to See   48
3. Discerning Different Atmospheres: Part 1   50
4. Discerning Atmospheres: Part 2   51
5. Discerning in the Nations   54

CHAPTER 6
Positioned to Perceive   57

ACTIVATE   60
1. What is Your Fragrance?   60
2. What Am I Dressed In?   62
3. Step into your new shoes   63
4. The Lion's Roar!   65
5. Who are you for me today, Jesus?   66

CHAPTER 7
Positioned in Expectation   71

ACTIVATE   76
1. What's Behind the Door?   76
2. Everyday Superheroes!   77
3. Lean Back   79
4. Change of Season!   81
5. God is Greater!   83

CHAPTER 8
Positioned in Heavenly Places ... 87
    ACTIVATE ... 89
    1. Intimacy is The Doorway to Heaven ... 89
    2. Come Up Higher! ... 90
    3. Heaven's Library ... 91
    4. Sacred Space ... 93
    5. News Flash ... 95

CHAPTER 9
Positioned in the Word ... 99
    ACTIVATE ... 100
    1. Throne Room Encounter ... 100
    2. Rest for your Soul ... 103
    3. House of God, the Gate of Heaven – You're it! ... 106
    4. Strengthen Yourself in the Lord ... 109
    5. Psalm 25 and a Path ... 111

CHAPTER 10
Positioned for Impact ... 115
    ACTIVATE ... 116
    1. Keys! ... 116
    2. God's Heavenly Solutionaries! ... 118
    3. Cry out for the Nations – Go to the Nations ... 120
    4. Declarations for Nations ... 123
    5. Releasing Heaven's Joy ... 125

ACTIVATE BONUS
Christmas Activation: The Christmas Gift ... 127
Easter Activation: Good Friday – Resurrection Power ... 128

Final Words ... 131

Introduction

Before this book was even a thought in my heart, a lot of these activations were birthed from a place of very personal encounters that I had with Holy Spirit in my own secret place, over many years. They came out of intimacy and friendship with Him. I didn't even know a word like 'activation' existed! They just happened when I spent time with Jesus and made room for Holy Spirit. I had a longing to encounter Him and it was right there that He met me. Holy Spirit will always meet you at your hunger. So right there in my hunger and hiddenness, Holy Spirit began to teach me about the realm of the spirit. He opened my eyes to 'see' and took me into all sorts of encounters that are treasured in my many, many journals. And as far as I knew, I thought they were just for me.

Then one day He opened a door for me to lead others through them too and, to my absolute joy, many began to tell me how these little activations were impacting and transforming their spiritual lives.

The heart behind writing this book was to design a simple but powerful tool to put into the hands of everyday people who have a desire to go after the 'more' of God and grow in accessing the realm of the spirit. 'Make room for more' is a catch-cry I live by, so these activations became another way that I could equip and empower others to do that.

The activations you'll find in this book have all been used in one way or another, in our Supernatural School of Ministry – School of Faith, by our leaders and students across the nations. They have led so many people into genuine, life-changing, Holy Spirit encounters and have helped sharpen their spiritual senses in the process.

My prayer is that this book will activate you and set you in motion on a journey of leading yourself, your family, your church, your ministry, or your mission-field (wherever that may be) into Holy Spirit encounters that become your new normal.

Don't be surprised if some of the deepest and most profound encounters you have, come from these very activations!

ACTIVATE

At the end of every chapter, you will find a section called 'Activate'. This is where you get to practise engaging and encountering the realm of the spirit. Activations are simple steps to engage in guided encounters with Father, Son and Holy Spirit. Each activation requires you to find a space where you can be without distractions.

Matthew 6:6 gives us a great Biblical address to position ourselves for encounters: the Secret Place.

> *"But you, when you pray, go into your room,*
> *and when you have shut your door, pray to your Father*
> *who is in the secret place; and your Father*
> *who sees in secret will reward you openly."*
> *Matthew 6:6 (NKJV)*

Remember that you may hear, see, feel or know things in the spirit realm and these activations are going to help you practise tuning in to the way Holy Spirit speaks uniquely to YOU!

All activations can be done as an individual or in a group setting. Each 'Activate' section will have a group section and that group can be anything from 2 people up to 100! The Group Activation will vary depending on the activation. Some are longer than others. Find what works for your group.

When doing this as a group, it is important that everyone can get comfortable and focus their attention on Jesus and listen to Holy Spirit individually first, without distractions. A leader will have to guide the group through the activation, by reading the steps out loud. Be sure to pace it and give people time to enter in and encounter what you are leading them through. A good tip is to lead yourself through the encounter as you lead others through it. This way you not only get a realistic gauge of timing, but also get blessed in the process. It might be helpful to put the activation steps up on a screen, although it is not essential for the activation to work.

Playing instrumental worship or soaking music softly in the background can help set the atmosphere, whether you are on your own or in a group. I would suggest using worship music that doesn't have lyrics as they can distract or interfere with the encounter. The music should be there to help people focus and tune into the Presence of Holy Spirit. The goal is always encounter.

I recommend you have a journal ready to write down or draw all that you hear and see during your encounters. This is how we steward our learning and experiences, which in turn sharpens our senses. There is something beautiful about being able to record such precious and powerful moments.

Help! What do I do if things go wrong?

Some of us have experienced measures of brokenness and trauma in our lives. There are times when we may be going through an activation that might trigger painful memories or reveal brokenness that is still hidden and present within our hearts and lives.

The premise for each activation is that Father, Son and Holy Spirit are good, and they are safe. They not only release love, peace and joy – they are Love, Peace and Joy. The goal in each encounter is to grow more in love with Jesus, tune into the voice of the Father and walk in step with Holy Spirit. The impetus behind each activation is to strengthen, encourage and comfort you (1 Corinthians 14:3 NLT). Although there can be a 'stretch' in the activation, it should never lead to a place of pain, fear, darkness, or confusion.

If you find that happens to you, STOP! Take a deep breath and come out of the encounter. Ask Holy Spirit what, why and where the pain or fear is coming from. Maybe there is an area in your life or heart that He is wanting to bring healing or restoration to. Allow Him to do that. He is so committed to your wholeness.

If it is something deeper than you feel you can work through by yourself, reach out to a trusted Christian leader or friend, or even a counsellor. There are times we cannot do this alone, and God has the right people in place to journey with us to freedom and wholeness.

Now, are you ready? Let the adventure begin …

CHAPTER 1

Positioned for Presence

*"And God raised us up with Christ and seated us
with Him in the heavenly realms in Christ Jesus."*
Ephesians 2:6 (NIV)

Our 'normal' according to the Bible, is heavenly realms. That means we get to see and encounter heavenly places and spaces. Did you know that you are a dual citizen? The Kingdom of heaven is just as much our home as earth is.

As mysterious as it is, this is not just a theological belief or a mere idea or concept but a literal reality. Holy Spirit says to you right now: "I am declaring 'Access Supplied'". When it comes to heavenly realms, or heavenly places, so many of us live as though it's 'Access Denied' but that is a lie! The Bible tells us we are seated right there with Christ Jesus!

Jesus declared that He only did what He saw the Father doing and said what He heard the Father saying (John 5:19). Jesus perfectly modelled how to live this way. As we walk on this earth in all of our humanity, we can be simultaneously connected to heavenly places – the realm of the spirit, so that we are seeing and hearing what is going on there and then doing that here. That is how we do 'on earth as it is in heaven.'

We need to learn to train our senses, just like it says in Hebrews 5:14.

*"But solid food is for the mature, who by constant use
have trained their senses to distinguish good from evil."*
(BSB)

Our senses matter and the best thing is that our senses can be trained to become fully alert and engaged in the realm of the spirit.

God loves all of our senses. He created them, He redeemed, and is continuing to redeem, them and He wants us to ongoingly experience Him with ALL of them – natural and spiritual.

He also wants us to have our senses trained so that He can encounter us in personal, tangible, genuine, manifested, very real ways. He wants us to learn to recognise His face, His voice, His sound, His smell and His touch. This is an invitation to a love encounter. Once you 'taste and see' that He is so good, you'll never be the same again!

Pray this with me right now: **"Holy Spirit, I ask that you come and awaken every one of my natural and spiritual senses to your Presence. Make me sensitised to You. I want more! Stir in me a holy discontent so that I won't settle for less than what you promised and less than what is available. I choose to go after it all! Adjust and align me to be 'normal' according to Your normal. In Jesus Name, Amen!"**

Get ready for upgrades into your new normal. Once you begin to encounter His Presence you will never be able to settle for anything less!

ACTIVATE

1. Come as a Child — What's the Game?

Fun is an important way that Jesus shows us His Father's love. It is part of Jesus' message that the all-powerful, all-knowing God is *our Abba, our dear Papa, our Father, our Dad!* Think about that for a moment! (Mark 14:36, Romans 8:15, Galatians 4:6).

Jesus tells us that we must become like little children to come into the Kingdom. Some versions of the bible say to inherit the Kingdom. We all want to walk in the fullness of our Kingdom inheritance and a key is becoming like children. Not childish but child-like!

Activation

> 1. Take a moment to focus in on the Presence of the Lord. Surrender to Him and tune into His Love for you. Breathe that in and let every other thing go as you exhale.
> 2. Pray this prayer over yourself or over your group:

3. "I break off all limitations and religiosity in Jesus name and release you/myself to be like a 'child'! I pray that you/I will have a fun and powerfully releasing experience with Jesus today! That as you/I enjoy Him; weariness, heaviness, and the 'weight' of responsibilities and worries will come off and you/I will encounter new levels of freedom in the Mighty Name of Jesus! Amen!

4. Invite Holy Spirit to come and reveal Jesus to you. He is going to come and sit with you. Where is He in relation to you? Is He in front of you? Or next to you?

5. Now ask Jesus, 'What game do you want us to play together?' A game might immediately come to mind. Or Jesus might hold out a game to you – like cards or a skipping rope. Maybe it's snakes and ladders or hide and seek? The options are endless!
   * If you are struggling to 'see or hear' anything, pick a game that was one of your favourites growing up.

6. Ask Jesus, 'Why do you want to play this game? What does it mean for my life? What is your heart intention through it, towards me?'

7. See yourself playing the game with Jesus! How does it feel? What is Jesus like when He plays with you?

8. Write down or draw a picture of your experience.

Groups

1. Leader: you may want to play some instrumental worship music softly in the background.

2. Read through the above activation. Be sure to pace it so that people can engage with the activation and encounter what Holy Spirit is saying and showing them.

3. Be sure to give them time to write and/or draw what He has shown them.

4. Have everyone share their experience with a partner.

5. Come back as a whole group and have 2 or 3 share why it was so meaningful or significant to them.

6. Leader: Pray for the group that they receive child-like faith, joy and wonder again.

2. Heaven's Waterfall

"Deep calls to deep at the roar of your waterfalls…"
Psalm 42:7 (ESV)

Activation

1. Quiet yourself before God and imagine standing under a huge waterfall. Ask Holy Spirit to pour down on you.

2. Whilst standing under that imaginary waterfall, ask Holy Spirit to help you tangibly see/hear or feel something from Him.

3. Now ask Him to give you fresh hope for an impossible situation in your life.

4. Ask Holy Spirit to give you a Bible verse or reassurance that He has heard you.

5. Now, ask Holy Spirit to bring someone you know to your mind. Ask Him to give you a picture/word/verse that will release hope to that person.

6. Send them a text/message/voice message/call with what you got and bless them today!

Groups

1. Leader: you may want to play some instrumental worship music softly in the background.

2. Read through the above activation. Be sure to pace it so that people can engage with the activation and encounter what Holy Spirit is saying and showing them.

3. Be sure to give them time to write and/or draw what He has shown them.
4. Have everyone hold up their phones and release hope over every person that came to mind and commission each participant to release what Holy Spirit has shown/given them.
5. Allow time within the session for participants to send a text/message/voice message.
6. Then have people come up and share what they got in their group.

3. Road Trip with Jesus!

Some of the best times of heart-to-heart conversations I've had with my kids have happened in the car (especially the teenagers!).

I felt Holy Spirit invite each of us on a road-trip with Jesus where He wanted to share heart-to-heart with us.

Activation

1. Quiet yourself before the Lord and ask Holy Spirit to help you tune in to Him.
2. You are invited to go on a road trip with Jesus today!
3. What is the vehicle He is inviting you into? (It could be a car; bus; train; aeroplane …anything! Let Him show you!).
4. Look at the details. Ask Holy Spirit to show you 'why' that vehicle; why that colour? God is in the details!
5. Now see yourself sitting next to Jesus and ask Him 'What do you want to share with me on this road trip?'
6. Write down or draw what He tells you.

Groups

1. Leader: you may want to play some instrumental worship music softly in the background.

2. Read through the above activation. Be sure to pace it so that people can engage with the activation and encounter what Holy Spirit is saying and showing them.

3. Be sure to give them time to write and/or draw what He has shown them.

4. Partner up and share your experience with each other.

4. Picnic with Jesus

The other day as I spent time in my secret place, Jesus met me on a track we have been to before. It is a bush track and we have walked it many times together. As we began to walk up the track, I assumed we were going to our 'usual' spot, however this time Jesus led me through some shrubs and suddenly we were on a beach! We walked onto the sand and Jesus put out a picnic rug.

I sat there with Jesus, listening to the waves and breathing in the fresh sea air. It was so refreshing! Then Jesus brought out a small container and opened the lid. In it were what looked like small red berries but they were unlike anything I've ever seen before. Then He began to feed me! I wondered why and He said that He wanted to give me something that would nourish and sustain my soul.

It was the most precious time!

Activation

1. Quiet your heart and mind down and welcome Holy Spirit. Breathe in His Presence deeply.

2. Now picture yourself on a path outside: is it in a garden? Is it a bush track? Is it in a forest? On a hill or in a valley?

3. Jesus meets you there and you begin to walk down the path/track together. What are you aware of in the surroundings? Is there anything He says to you?

4. Jesus leads you to a spot where He wants to set up a picnic. Where is that? What does it look like? How does He set up your picnic?

5. What does it feel like to be there? Listen to the sounds and smell the air. Breathe in deeply.

6. What does Jesus want to feed you or give you to drink? Look at the details – He is always in the details! Ask questions if you need to.

7. Is there anything Jesus does or wants you to know?

8. Be sure to write down or draw everything you get and then thank Him for such a special time.

Groups

1. Leader: take people through the above activation. Be sure to pace it so that people have time to encounter Jesus.

2. You may want to play some soaking music softly in the background to help people switch off to distractions and tune into Presence.

3. Have 2 or 3 people share their experience with the whole group.

5. The Secret Garden

"I have entered my garden, my treasure, my bride! ..."
Song of Solomon 5:1 (NLT)

As I spent time in worship, I had a beautiful encounter with Jesus in a Secret Garden. It was so pretty and so full of life and peace. We sat together on a little white garden chair, and I was completely at rest. I began to ask Jesus questions like 'What do you want to tell me? What is on your heart?' But He simply smiled and I knew, without Him saying the words out loud, that He wanted us to just 'be' together. To sit as best friends or lovers do – no words needed. Just intimate friendship! It was there, in that place of absolute bliss that Jesus reached out and handed me something so precious ...

Activation

1. Find a place where you can be alone with Jesus (Secret Place – Matthew 6:6).

2. Quiet your soul (mind, will and emotions) and invite Holy Spirit to come! He loves to reveal Jesus!

3. In your imagination space or with the eyes of your heart, see yourself with Jesus in a beautiful garden. What does it look like? What can you see there? How do you feel being there?

4. Sit with Jesus. Where does He want to sit with you (it could be a park bench or a garden swing or on a picnic rug – remember there are no limitations).

5. Now look at Jesus. Lean in close to Him. Breathe in deeply and enjoy just *being* together with Him.

6. Jesus wants to give you something. Open up your hands with expectation. What is it that He is placing into your hands? Ask Holy Spirit to tell you about it!

7. Write it down. This is part of stewarding and valuing our encounters.

Groups

1. Leader: take people through the above activation. Be sure to pace it so that people have time to encounter Jesus.

2. You may want to play some soaking music softly in the background to help people switch off to distractions and tune into Presence.

3. Have people share their experience either in pairs or in smaller groups of 3-4.

CHAPTER 2

Positioned for More

Throughout the whole Bible we see evidence of a God who loves us so much that He has made a way for us to ongoingly encounter the 'more' of His Presence. He always chooses to come near. He wants us to experience Him in our humanity. We are designed to encounter and enjoy Him!

I want to share something with you that I hope will free some of you and give you permission to begin to encounter Him on every level.

2 Corinthians 5:17 is one of my all-time favourite scriptures and the very first scripture that I learnt when I gave my life to Jesus all those years ago.

It says this: *"Therefore, if anyone is in Christ, he {or she} is a new creation. The old has passed away; behold, the new has come." (ESV)*

Did you get that? The Bible says we have become brand new creations! The 'old has gone, completely, and the new has come'.

It is not a 'do-over' or a 'glow-up' but a complete redo! We die to our old lives, and we become alive to Christ. A metamorphosis takes place! We come out of the cocoon of death and emerge completely brand new.

This means that if we are completely new creations, then every part of us has been made new, including our soul, which is our mind, will and emotions.

Our souls, as well as our bodies, have been redeemed and sanctified just as much as our spirits. Yes, there is a process of sanctification – of the 'now' and the 'not yet', but Holy Spirit is committed to making this an ongoing reality as He transforms us into the very image of Jesus!

It's from 'glory to glory' that we go.
Increasing measure of glory, that's our story!

We have a great ongoing invitation into the 'more' that God has for each of us. He wants us to encounter His Presence and when we do, that means all of us - body, soul and spirit. Have a look at Matthew 22:37 (BSB)

> *"Teacher, which commandment is the greatest in the Law?"*
> *<u>Jesus declared, "'Love the Lord your God with all your heart and with all your soul and with all your mind.'</u> This is the first and greatest commandment..."*

Let's have a look at a couple of the keywords here in the Greek:

Mind: **dianoia** or **dianous** = deep thought, imagination, understanding.[1]

We can see here clearly that our 'mind' refers not only to logical understanding but also the area of *deep thought and* imagination.

Do you get what this means? This is permission to engage our thoughts as well as our imagination!

How do we love Him with our *deep thoughts and imagination?*

That has to look like something. There has to be an outward expression of encounter in the areas of our mind and imagination.

The posture of our heart allows us to position ourselves to receive the 'more' that Holy Spirit has for us.

A few years ago, we were having a short holiday at a gorgeous little house on a rural property in Victor Harbor, South Australia. We were surrounded by rolling hills, neighbouring alpacas, kangaroos and the majestic Aussie bush. I woke up early and went out to the verandah to pray. There is something so special about encountering the nearness of Jesus when you are surrounded by nature.

As I worshipped and sat with Jesus, I looked out and suddenly the surroundings in the bush in front of me began to shift. The natural became superimposed by the supernatural. Every tree, leaf and flower began to vibrate and pulsate with life on another level! A great wonder and fear came upon me as heaven literally touched earth. I had a thought that this was perhaps a complete other dimension that I was seeing. An overwhelming awareness of Jesus' Presence was all around and every sense in me was awakened and on high alert. In fact, I had the strongest impression that if I had walked over and into what was happening out in front of me, I would walk from this earth into eternity! It felt like a crossing-point between heaven and earth. I had never had anything like this happen before and have never had it since. It was profound and deeply marked me.

---

[1] https://biblehub.com/greek/1271.htm

As we posture ourselves in His Presence – fully surrendered on every level; body, soul and spirit; where loving Him is our goal, then we are perfectly positioned for the radical 'suddenlies' of the more of God to break in on us, around us and through us.

This is the great invitation of Holy Spirit: 'Come! Dive into the deep and let Me take you into realms of My Presence that will not only mark you but will transform you from glory to glory.'

ACTIVATE

1. Dad's Toolbox

> *"Call to me and I will show you great and hidden things that you have not known."*
> Jeremiah 33:3 (ESV)

Activation

1. Welcome Holy Spirit and begin to lean into His Presence (lean in simply means to come near, as though you were listening to a whisper). Become aware of Him.
2. Now Jesus is coming to you with a toolbox. It is from the Father. What does it look like? What colour is it? Is it heavy or light?
3. Ask Him: What tool do you want to give me today that will help the church grow in this season and why?
4. Write down the tool you see/get/hear/sense – e.g. hammer, and the details you see on it.
5. Write down what He says about it. What is it for; Why? Remember to ask questions.
6. Now turn it into a decree and declare it!

7. Have an expectation that things will shift; angels will be dispatched; strongholds will break; and heaven will be released as you decree what He has said.

Groups

1. Leader: take people through the above activation. Be sure to pace it so that people have time to encounter Jesus.
2. You may want to play some soaking music softly in the background to help people switch off to distractions and tune into Presence.
3. Have people come out one by one and release those declarations/decrees over the whole group. This is how we partner with Holy Spirit.

2. Where in the World?

> *"Ask of Me and I will make the nations your inheritance, the ends of the earth your possession…"*
> Psalm 2:8 (NIV)

A while ago I was in prayer and Holy Spirit said, "If you sow to the nations, you will go to the nations."

I was excited! His heart is for all nations to reach all nations and He wants to use you and I. We can sow in many different ways; with our time, our money, our prayers and our talents. This activation is about partnering with Holy Spirit for the nations in prayer.

Activation

1. Quiet yourself and invite Holy Spirit to increase His Presence and your awareness of Him right now.
2. Now ask Him: if He could take you anywhere in the world right now, where would He take you and why?

3. Capture that first thought that goes through your mind, or the first thing you feel or see.
4. Ask Holy Spirit some more questions about that place:
5. "Why did you pick that place?"
6. "What's special about that place?"
7. "Holy Spirit, what do you want to say to me here in this place you've chosen for me?"
8. "Is there something you want me to pray or declare over that city or nation?"
9. Take time to do that right now.
10. Write down all He has shown you.

Groups

1. Leader: take people through the activation. Be sure to pace it so that people have time to encounter Jesus.
2. You may want to play some soaking music softly in the background to help people switch off to distractions and tune into Presence.
3. After the activation, go round the whole group and get each person to call out the nations that Holy Spirit showed them during the activation.
4. Take note of any common nations that Holy Spirit was speaking into.
5. Based on the feedback you just received, put the people who got the same nation into a corner/corners of the room to lead those groups. For example, if 2 or more people got Spain, then create a group called 'Spain' in one corner; if 2 or more people got India, create another group called 'India' and put them in another corner. Depending on how many people you have in your whole group, you could do this for 4 nations or more. The groups should not be bigger than 6-8 people.

6. Now invite the rest of the wider group to join one of the nations represented.

7. Have the leaders in the groups share what Holy Spirit gave/said/showed them in relation to that nation.

8. Have each group partner with Holy Spirit in relation to what He showed them and spend some time interceding for that nation.

Note: If there were no nations/cities repeated in the group, then as a leader, choose 1-4 (depending on the size of your group) nations/cities that stand out to you and follow the same steps above.

The aim is to practise partnering with what Holy Spirit shows us prophetically through intercession.

3. Let's Go Fruit Picking

Activation

1. In your imagination space with Holy Spirit, I want you to see yourself in a heavenly garden full of fruit trees. Jesus is with you!

2. Look around! What do you see? What fruit do you see on the trees?

3. Ask Jesus to show you which fruit He wants you to have. Go to the tree and either let Jesus give it to you or pick it yourself. Look and take note of the detail (e.g. golden apple).

4. Ask Jesus: 'What does this fruit represent?' (e.g., a golden apple might mean an invitation into sweet, glorious intimacy).

5. Write down what fruit you picked or were given and what Jesus told you.

6. Surprise! THIS FRUIT IS FOR SOMEONE ELSE! (Although it may also be for you too.)

7. Who is this for? Ask Holy Spirit who He wants you to share this with and make time to do that either right now or during this week.

Groups

1. Leader: take the people through this activation. Be sure to pace it so that people have time to encounter Jesus.

2. You may want to play some soaking music softly in the background to help people switch off to distractions and tune into Presence.

3. Have everyone share their fruit and as they do, ask them to give it to someone in the group and bless them as they do. For example, 'Holy Spirit gave me a golden apple and He said it is for… And I believe I need to give it to … because … So I bless you with that in Jesus Name.'

4. Treasure Box

One day as I was spending time in worship, I saw a picture of a treasure box. I felt Jesus immediately say: "I'm coming with the Treasure Box of heaven to gift my people!"

Jesus has hand-picked treasures for you! These treasures are for your NOW season. I heard the words "upgrade" and I believe that He wants to give you something specific that will be an upgrade in who you are called to be NOW.

Activation

1. Ask Holy Spirit to show you the Treasure Box and open it up! Take a moment to look at the details.

2. Ask Him to give you the gift Jesus has chosen for you.

3. Again, look at the details and be specific.

4. Write down what it is and ask Him what it means/what it is for.
5. Take it – literally, as a prophetic act – and put it on or pick it up.
6. Journal/draw what you have received and thank Him for it.

Groups

1. Leader: take the group through the activation. Be sure to pace it so that people have time to encounter Jesus.
2. You may want to play some soaking music softly in the background to help people switch off to distractions and tune into Presence.
3. Go around the group and ask each person to share what they received.
4. Ask the group: 'Who would like this also, or needs this in their life right now?'
5. Have the person go to those who responded and prophetically give the gift to them. Pray to impart the treasure into their life.

5. Cave of Wonders

The cave in the classic Disney story Aladdin was called the 'Cave of Wonders'. Did you know that Aladdin's name is an English version of Al-al-Din which means *nobility of faith*?

That is who we are! We are nobility – sons and daughters of the King! We are princes and princesses of faith!

Holy Spirit is putting out an invitation for you to come and enter the heavenly 'Cave of Wonders' with Him and see the treasures He has stored up for you.

Activation

1. Close your eyes and invite Holy Spirit to come and fill your mind. Connect in with His Presence.
2. See yourself standing at the Cave of Wonders and go in.
3. What does it look like in there? What can you see? What can you touch?
4. Journal what you are seeing and experiencing or draw a picture of it.
5. Ask Holy Spirit what He wants you to take. What is it? Why this object? (It might be a precious jewel or gemstone; it might be a crown or a sword or even a golden chalice…).
6. What does it look like and what is it for? What does it symbolise? What does it mean for your 'now' situation? Remember to ask for details!
7. How does this equip you for what is happening right now in your life, whether it be in your personal life, your family, your church, or your workplace.
8. Holy Spirit has a purpose for this special gift that will increase your faith.
9. Take time to thank Him for what He has given you.

Groups

1. Leader: take the whole group through the activation. Be sure to pace it so that people have time to encounter Jesus.
2. You may want to play some soaking music softly in the background to help people switch off to distractions and tune into Presence.
3. Now have another look around the cave and ask Holy Spirit for something you can give away to someone else.
4. Ask Holy Spirit what He wants you to take. What is it? Why this object? (It might be a precious jewel or gemstone; it might be a crown or a sword or even a golden chalice…).

5. What does it look like and what is it for? What does it symbolise? Remember to ask for details!

6. How will this equip them for what is happening right now in their life, whether it be in their personal life, family, church, or workplace.

7. Ask everyone to write down or draw what the gift means to them and symbolises for them. If you draw a picture, be sure to label it with specific details.

8. Leader: have everyone go to another person in the group and share what they saw or got.

9. Give what you were given from the cave to the person you are partnered with; ask for feedback.

10. Pray for an impartation of faith to be released.

CHAPTER 3

Positioned in Love

Going back to our scripture in Matthew 22:37, let's continue to look at what loving the Lord with all our 'soul' looks like.

The word for soul here in this case is **psuché**: which means 'the seat of our affections and will.'

Did you see that the word for 'soul' not only speaks of the mind or will, but also refers to the seat of our affections?

So then, let's unpack that scripture a little further. Loving the Lord with our soul literally includes our mind and our affection. This encompasses:

▶ our understanding and our deep thoughts, which are the meditations of the heart;

▶ our imagination, which is our creative and dream centre;

▶ our affections and emotions, which includes what we feel;

▶ and our will, which is our decision centre.

What sort of a lover has no emotions? What sort of love is it if I cannot feel it or show it? What sort of love is it if I did not have a choice in it? Lovers are dreamers. Lovers are willing to pay whatever the price to be with the one they love. Lovers will passionately shout it from the rooftop "I am in LOVE"!

That does not happen because of an intellectual assent to the notion of love. Sure, there comes a time when there has to be more than just feelings and that is when our will comes into effect. We do not base love purely on feelings but also on a decision. We choose to love. We as humans are empowered to make decisions through an act of our will, and our mind and emotions will follow. But it is never at the expense of our feelings or imaginations.

We are to love Him with everything! He gave His all and now we get to give our all to Him.

In the book of Revelation, there is a clear and sharp message to the church at Ephesus:

> *"Nevertheless, I have this against you,*
> *that you have left your first love."*
> Revelation 2:4 (NKJV)

Can you see clearly how seriously God takes our love for Him?

Some of you reading this right now, have shut down your emotions because of the fear of 'emotionalism.' For others, you were wrongly taught that emotions are evil or a sign of weakness or inappropriate for church or your relationship with Jesus. Others of you have shut them down to protect your heart because of pain, trauma, or disappointment. Holy Spirit wants to heal you and awaken you to first love. And lastly, a big amount of churchgoing, good Christians simply do not burn with love for Jesus on any level. They have become inoculated or numb because of familiarity. Holy Spirit wants to bring healing, freedom and deliverance right now. He wants to awaken your emotions to first love! He wants to baptise you with love – right now, before we go on to anything else.

Firstly, if you need to, repent. That means say sorry for shutting down your emotions; for letting fear get in the way; for judging others for seemingly being 'emotional'; for anything else Holy Spirit brings to mind. Repent literally means, 'change the way you think.'

Secondly, you may need to forgive, yourself or others, for hurting you. Ask Holy Spirit to show you if this is something you need to do. Unforgiveness is an emotional blocker and will be an unhealthy and unhelpful filter over your heart if not dealt with.

Thirdly, renounce the lie that says emotions are inappropriate, evil, at odds with faith or anything else that Holy Spirit shows you.

Take a deep breath!

Now pray this with me out loud:

"Thank you, Father, for creating me as an emotional being. I am made like you, in Your likeness and You have emotions! You designed me with them and said, "It is good!"

Right now, I call my emotions up to the surface in Jesus' name and say, "Wake up!"
I bless my emotions to function the way God designed them to.
Bring healing and wholeness to them Lord.

(Put your hand on your heart)

And I invite you Holy Spirit to awaken me to first love.
Baptise me with your love right here, right now, in Jesus Name.
I receive it!
Amen!"

ACTIVATE

1. Invitation to go on a Date

> *"The one I love calls to me*
> *Arise, my dearest. Hurry, my darling.*
> *Come away with me!*
> *I have come as you have asked*
> *to draw you to my heart and lead you out.*
> *For now is the time, my beautiful one"*
> *Song of Solomon 2:10 TPT*

Activation

1. Find a quiet place and still your soul (mind, will and emotions). Invite Holy Spirit to come and quiet you with His love.

2. In this place I want you to see Jesus coming to you. He has a rose in His hand to give you and He is inviting you on a 'one-on-one' date with Him.

3. Where does Jesus want to take you? What has He got planned for you on this date? Is there anything He wants you to leave or to bring with you?

4. Go with Him! Where are you? What did Jesus prepare for you to enjoy there? What is the scenery or setting?

5. Ask Him if there is anything He wants to share with you or say to you as you spend time together.

6. How did you feel being with Jesus on this date? How has He surprised you or how have you changed from this time with Him?

7. Ask Him for one word from Him that describes who you are to Him (e.g., Beloved; Precious; Priceless…etc).

Groups

1. Leader: lead the whole group through the activation. Be sure to pace it so that people have time to encounter Jesus.

2. You may want to play some soaking music softly in the background to help people switch off to distractions and tune into Presence.

3. Share about your experience in this activation with a partner.

4. Tell them the word that Jesus spoke over you.

5. Pray for each other, releasing that identity word.

6. If there is time, bring the group back together and have 1 or 2 share with the whole group.

2. The Banquet Table

> "He brought me to the banqueting house hall
> and His banner over me is love."
> Song of Solomon 2:4 (NASB)

Activation

1. There's something about sharing a meal with someone that you love.
2. Today there is an invitation from the Beloved, King Jesus, to come to the banqueting hall and feast under His banner of love.
3. Find a place to quiet your soul (mind, will and emotions). Invite Holy Spirit into that space with you. Just like we have natural senses, so too do we have spiritual senses. We can see, hear, touch and smell in the realm of the spirit.
4. (Groups: leader to pray over the whole group before beginning and invite Holy Spirit to breathe on and awaken people's spiritual senses).
5. Invite Holy Spirit to show you Jesus and the banqueting table that He is inviting you to.
6. What does it look like? How is Jesus dressed for the occasion? Where is He? What is on the table? Remember to look at the details and ask questions.
7. Sit down with Jesus at the table. Where are you sitting? Where is He in relation to you? What does He serve you? Can you smell it? What does it taste like?
8. As you enjoy your time at the table with Jesus ask Him what is on His heart. Intimate mealtimes are often times to share heart to heart.
9. Does the 'banner of His love' over you look or feel like something? If so, describe it. (You may see something, or you may simply know or feel something – all are valid)
10. Write it down or draw a picture.
11. What does it feel like under that banner of love? Take a moment to allow yourself to engage in it with your senses – natural and/or spiritual. If you could describe it in words, what would you say?

Groups

> 1. Leader: lead the whole group through the above activation. Be sure to pace it so that people have time to encounter Jesus.
> 2. You may want to play some soaking music softly in the background to help people switch off to distractions and tune into Presence.
> 3. After the activation, have everyone stand together in a circle facing each other.
> 4. Have individuals take turns to share briefly about their encounter at the banqueting table with Jesus.
> 5. If the group is large (more than 12), create 2 or more circles.
> 6. After each has shared, now invite some to share about the 'banner of love'. What did that look and feel like?
> 7. Have them release that over the group.
> 8. Encourage everyone to take a moment to stand in it and feel what that feels like.
> 9. Invite people to share what they felt as the banner of love was released over them.

3. God's Glory Box

As I spent time with Jesus in the secret place, I felt Holy Spirit whisper 'Glory Box'.

Did you know that a glory box is also called a 'hope box'? A glory box is an old-fashioned idea where a young girl collects items that will be helpful for her in marriage. I felt Holy Spirit say that He wants to present each of us our 'glory box'. This is a box of His glory! He has things to give each of us in preparation for our bridegroom Jesus! For some of you, this is your 'hope box'. You need hope in the season you are in.

God wants to release His glory to us today! Moses cried out "…show me Your glory…" (Exodus 33:18).

In today's activation, you are invited to encounter His glory and when you do, you get to become a carrier and releaser of that very glory!

Activation

1. Find a spot where you can be with the Lord. Go to your secret place. Take a moment to focus your love and attention on Jesus and invite Holy Spirit to come and fill the space.
2. Ask Holy Spirit to show you your 'glory box'. Remember that God is in the details! Look at the box. What details do you see? What is it made of? Is it big or small? Is there any writing on it or engraving? What colour is it?
3. Open your box. What is inside? What is there for you to take? Ask questions like 'why' and 'what is it for'? Then take time to thank Him!

Groups

1. Leader: lead the whole group through the above activation. Be sure to pace it so that people have time to encounter Jesus.
2. You may want to play some soaking music softly in the background to help people switch off to distractions and tune into Presence.
3. Once the activation has finished, have people come up one at a time, and share what they got from their glory box. After sharing their personal encounter, have each one stay standing and ask Holy Spirit to highlight one other person in the group. Have them ask that person to stand up. (Only take seconds or a minute to do this).
4. Ask Holy Spirit what He wants to give that person from the glory box and then release it to them.
5. They might pray over them or do a prophetic act to 'give' them what they got.

4. May We Never Lose the Wonder

I love the lyrics of this Bethel song:

> *"Wide-eyed and mystified, may we be just like a child, staring at the beauty of our King. May we never lose the wonder!"*
> – Wonder by Bethel Music and Amanda Cook

That is my prayer for you today. That you would re-discover the wonder of what it is to love Jesus. Simple!

Activation

1. Go to your secret place and invite Holy Spirit to come in you and on you. There's an invitation for Holy Spirit to bring child-like wonder into your life. Invite Him to do that right now.
2. Using your imagination, see yourself as a child standing in front of a big door that is slightly open. Picture yourself opening the door and taking a peek!
3. What does the door look like? What does it feel like opening that door up? Is there anything that surprises you or that is familiar to you?
4. Jesus is on the other side of the door! What do you see there? What does He look like? How do you feel looking at Him and being with Him?
5. What does Jesus do next? What does Jesus want to show you, take you to or give you to let you know He loves you?
6. Journal your experience – in words and/or pictures.

Groups

1. Leader has everyone find a space in the room.
2. You may want to play some instrumental worship music softly in the background.

3. Take everyone through the activation steps above. Be sure to pace it so that people have a chance to engage and encounter Jesus.
4. Allow time for everyone to write down and/or draw their encounter.
5. Ask the group to partner up to share their journaling and pray for each other.
6. Come back as a whole group and invite 1 or 2 to share with everyone.

5. Wrap Around Love

> *"Because I set you, Yahweh, always close to me,*
> *my confidence will never be weakened,*
> *for I experience your wraparound presence every moment.*
> *My heart and soul explode with joy—full of glory!*
> *Even my body will rest confident and secure."*
> *Psalm 16:8-9 (TPT)*

There is nothing like the wrap-around Presence of God! Think about that for a moment.

A new baby is swaddled and held close to his or her mum or dad. There is a peace, confidence and settled joy that comes with that. Safe and secure in the arms of the one who loves him or her more than anything in the world, close to their heartbeat!

In a world full of uncertainty, pain, fear and pressure, the Father wants to come to you today and wrap you up in His love.

Activation

1. Go to a place where you can be alone with the Father.
2. Invite Holy Spirit to increase your capacity to sense/feel/hear/see Him. I like to pray: "Wake up my senses Holy Spirit" or "Dial it up Lord!"

3. Now invite Him to bring His wrap-around-love to you. Wait for it! Practice becoming aware of what that feels like.
4. He is going to place something on you. It may be a shawl, it may be a blanket, or it may be a jacket or coat. Take note of what it is that the Lord is wrapping around you.
5. Remember, God is in the details, so have a look at the colour, what is the texture like or the feeling? Is there a weight? Or is it soft? Ask Him why.
6. Just 'be' in this place with His wrap-around Presence. How does it make you feel?
7. What is He saying/whispering/singing over you – His precious child?
8. Be sure to write down or draw all you encounter.

Groups

1. Leader: take the group through the activation steps above. Be sure to make room for people to engage and encounter.
2. Allow time to write down and/or draw what they experience.
3. In small groups of 3 or 4, share what you experienced and release His love to one another.

CHAPTER 4

Positioned to See

Moses was a great example of someone who was not content to just live with *head-knowledge* about God. He cried out for encounters and went after the 'more'. Everyone else pulled away and was happy to just acknowledge by faith that God was God. But not Moses! Moses cried out for God's glory and Presence above anything else. He went after an experience. Why? Because he dared to believe that it was available.

> *"So the LORD said to Moses, "I will do this very thing you have asked, for you have found favour in My sight, and I know you by name." Then Moses said, "Please show me Your glory …"*
> *Exodus 33:17-18 (BSB)*

The word for 'show' here in the original Hebrew language is *rā'â* – which literally means to see; to perceive; to have vision and to gaze at.

Moses wanted to see, perceive, have vision and gaze at God's glory! How audacious was that request?

This was before the Cross, where the veil was torn, and access was given to God's Presence. This should never have been a possibility. No-one saw God and lived! And yet, Moses dared to ask and God, in His lovingkindness, agreed. He let His glory pass before Moses so that he could 'see' Him in a way that would not kill him. That is how much He wants us to encounter Him!

I always say this, *"He will meet you at your hunger"*. This is what happened to Moses and what can happen for us too.

The Bible tells us that Moses met with God as a man meets with his friend, face to face. This is the intent of the heart of God – that His people would be a people who meet with Him face to face. What an invitation!

God wants to show Himself and His glory to His people. He is looking for those who are hungry and desperate enough to cry out: 'show me your glory'. He promises to draw near to those who draw near to Him. That looks like something! That feels like something!

It may be an encounter with glory that causes someone to shake, cry or laugh or it may be an overwhelming, reverential awe or weighty sense of His peace or love. Either way, He wants to be *known* by His sons and daughters.

In the Old Testament we read about a prophetic gift called the 'Seer Gift'. Samuel was a prophet who was a *'seer'*. A seer is basically someone who sees what is happening in the spiritual realm. They may see with their eyes open, or they may see within their mind or even see within a dream. Often, it's a combination.

The word we translate as seer is **chozeh**, and it is from the Hebrew word **chazah**, which means to see, to behold, to become aware, to become visible. It also means to experience.

Taste and see that I am good (Psalm 34:8 paraphrased). God Himself is always inviting His friends to see and experience Him. He wants our senses wide awake and receptive to His Presence.

There is an invitation for all of us to 'see' in this capacity. The invitation is there for us to come and see, to behold, become aware of, to perceive, to gaze upon and to experience everything that is of the realm of the spirit and His Presence.

Now that is a powerful and incredible offer! Who doesn't want that?

Here is a story that I absolutely love:

> *"When the servant of the man of God got up early the next morning and went outside, there were troops, horses, and chariots everywhere. "Oh, sir, what will we do now?" the young man cried to Elisha.*
>
> *"Don't be afraid!" Elisha told him. "For there are more on our side than on theirs!" Then Elisha prayed, "O Lord, open his eyes and let him see!" The Lord opened the young man's eyes, and when he looked up, he saw that the hillside around Elisha was filled with horses and chariots of fire.'*
> *2 Kings 6:15-17 NLT*

What a simple prayer! "O Lord, open his eyes and let him see!"

Why don't you pray that out loud, right now! "O Lord, open MY eyes and let ME see!"

ACTIVATE

1. Look to See!

What do you see?

> *"Then the LORD said to me, "Look, Jeremiah! What do you see? ..."*
> Jeremiah 1:11 (NLT)

Activation

Part 1: Personal Application

1. Look outside the window and ask God to highlight something to you. What is your eye drawn to? Is it a window or a bird, or a cloud or tree? Is it a billboard or even a car? It could be anything!

2. Now insert your name in the verse God said to Jeremiah: "Then the Lord said to me, "Look _____ (YOUR NAME)! What do you see?"

3. What is it that God wants to speak to you or tell you about, based on what you are 'seeing' or 'looking' at?

4. Look at the colour/shape/symbolism/words of what you are looking at. That will give prophetic 'clues' into what Holy Spirit is saying to you. You might get a Bible verse jump into your mind; or a knowing that bubbles up within you; maybe what you are seeing in the natural will launch you into a spiritual vision. Be open and be expectant!

5. Write or draw what you see and what you feel Holy Spirit is saying to you from that.

Groups

1. Leader: lead the whole group through the above activation. Be sure to pace it so that people have time to encounter Jesus.
2. You may want to play some soaking music softly in the background to help people switch off to distractions and tune into Presence.
3. Now follow the same activation but this time have people look on behalf of someone else in the group.
4. After they have done that, number everyone off to pair them up and have them release the word over each other.

Activation

Part 2: Personal Outreach

Now do the same thing:

1. Look outside the window and ask God to highlight something else to you. What is your eye drawn to?
2. Use that item as a basis to write a prophetic word for a friend/family member/someone from church. You can put it into a text or a card to give them.
3. Keep it simple and encouraging. God wants to share His love with them.
4. Send it to them in a text, or in a card or email (or just give them a call) to bless them today!

Groups

1. Leader: Have the 'Part 2: Outreach' section copied and/or printed out as handouts for each person in the group.

2. This part of the activation could be given as homework for each person in the group to take home and do in their own time.

3. Be sure to check in next time with the group to see how they went with the activation. Invite a few (if not all) to share.

2. Street Signs

Street Signs are very important and necessary.

They tell us where we are and how to get to where we are going. Today we are going to ask Holy Spirit to reveal a supernatural/heavenly street sign to us.

Activation

1. Ask God to reveal a street sign to you with the name of it (a real street name might come to mind or one unknown or made-up.). It might be a modern street sign or an old-fashioned one. Look at the detail.

2. Look at the word on the street sign.

3. What does it say? What colour is the sign?

4. Ask Holy Spirit why He revealed that street name to you. e.g., if you saw the word 'REST STREET', ask Him leading questions. Why did you show me this word/name? What does the colour mean? What do you want to lead me to and why?
This is what He said to me when I saw the name 'REST STREET': "My child, you have been so lost in a world of busyness lately. Follow the sign to find REST for your soul. I am taking you out of the rat-race and positioning you into the place of My REST".

5. Write down or draw what you got and make it a statement or declaration like the example given.

6. Now share it. Why don't you post your declaration

statement with a picture to match, on your socials? Or draw it down and then share it with a family member or friend.

Groups

1. Leader: lead the whole group through the above activation. Be sure to pace it so that people have time to encounter Jesus.
2. You may want to play some soaking music softly in the background to help people switch off to distractions and tune into Presence.
3. Have different people come up to share what their street sign is.
4. Invite those who need what is on that street sign to stand up (e.g., if the street sign is 'Freedom' and there are those needing freedom, invite them to stand up right now; if it is Rest Street and they want supernatural rest, stand up right now...).
5. Now have that person with the street sign release their declaration over those who are standing.

3. Revelation of Jesus – Look at His Face!

> *"Seek more of his strength! Seek more of him!*
> *Let's always be seeking the light of his face."*
> *Psalm 105:4 (TPT)*

Jesus is saying to you: 'Lift up your eyes and find my face. Find My face shining in glory, radiant like the sun, glowing in splendour and majesty. Lift up your eyes and find Me. Find Me gazing at your face, find Me looking into your eyes, find Me watching you, knowing you and experience Me today.

Look upon My passionate eyes of fire, look upon the flames of burning desire and love, feel the heat of the fire which burns in My eyes. Look at

My hair, white as snow, hear My voice speaking to you like the sounds of rushing water, see Me today. Lift up your gaze. I am making Myself known to you today.'

Activation

1. Find a quiet place – your secret place, where you can focus on Jesus.

2. Invite Holy Spirit to open your eyes and ears to the realm of the Spirit. Ask Him to reveal Jesus. He loves to do that!

3. Look upon the face of Jesus. Where is He in relation to you? What does He look like? How close is He to you? What do His eyes look like? Spend some time just looking there into His eyes.

4. Is there anything He wants to say to you or give you today? Or is there something He is saying with the gaze of His eyes?

5. Write down or draw your experience.

Groups

1. Leader: lead the whole group through the above activation. Be sure to pace it so that people have time to encounter Jesus.

2. You may want to play some soaking music softly in the background to help people switch off to distractions and tune into Presence.

3. Get into small groups of 4 or 5 and have each person share their experience with the group and pray for one another to encounter more.

4. The Banner

Activation

1. Quiet your heart and focus on Jesus. Invite Holy Spirit into your space and take a deep breath. Breathe in the atmosphere He is filling.
2. Then use your imagination and picture a plane flying overhead with a banner trailing behind it.
3. Look at the banner. What colour is it? What is the word or words that are written on it? Why?
4. Spend a few moments asking Holy Spirit more questions about the wording and what it means for you.
5. Write it down or draw what you see.
6. Then ask Holy Spirit to show you, in your imagination, the plane flying overhead again with a different banner. This time the banner is for someone else.
7. What colour and shape is it? What is written on it?
8. Ask Holy Spirit who it is for and why.
9. Is there anything else He wants to share with you about this?
10. Write it down or draw it on a piece of paper you can give away.

Groups

1. Leader: lead the whole group through the above activation. Be sure to pace it so that people have time to encounter Jesus.
2. You may want to play some soaking music softly in the background to help people switch off to distractions and tune into Presence.
3. Make time for everyone to find one person to share what they got for them.

OR

If you want to make this session more creative, bring in some paper, glitter, colour pencils or markers, pieces of fabric, ribbon etc., and have everyone 'create' the banner that Holy Spirit shows them. Then ask them to take this to prophesy over someone in the group and give the banner to them.

5. Royal Coronation

The Bible tells us that we are a 'royal priesthood'. We are royalty! He crowns us with lovingkindness! One day we will throw our crowns at His feet in worship and adoration. Today King Jesus wants to put a crown on your head. He is crowning you with, and for, a specific purpose.

Activation

1. Go to your secret place where you can shut out all distractions (Matthew 6:6).

2. Invite Holy Spirit to be there and to open your spiritual senses so you can be fully aware of and engaged with the realm of the spirit.

3. Ask Him to reveal Jesus. He loves to do this!

4. Where is Jesus in relation to you? Is He in front of you or next to you, or is He walking towards you? Can you see Him or feel His Presence? Take a moment to enjoy Him. Look at His face and His eyes. What do you feel as you do that?

5. Jesus has a crown to put on your head. What does it look like?

6. On this crown there is a word. What does it say? This is a word about your identity. It may be glory or honour or authority etc.

7. Allow Jesus to put the crown upon your head. Ask Him 'What is your purpose in this for me?'

8. Write down or draw what He has shown and what He tells you.

9. Take time to thank Him for the identity He has crowned you with today.

Groups

1. Leader: lead the whole group through the above activation. Be sure to pace it so that people have time to encounter Jesus.
2. You may want to play some soaking music softly in the background to help people switch off to distractions and tune into Presence.
3. Once the activation has finished, have each person share what they received with the whole group.
4. After sharing, have each person make an 'I am statement' based on what they were given and/or told by Jesus.
5. 'I am…' (Insert who you are based on what Jesus crowned you with.)
6. Make sure everyone celebrates each person (cheer, clap, make a big hoo-ha!) once they give their "I am" statement.
7. Be ready to minister as Holy Spirit shifts people out of old, broken identities and into His truth. This is going to be powerful for many.

CHAPTER 5

Positioned to Discern

'Look to see!'

Holy Spirit interrupted me during our worship time at church one Sunday. I knew immediately that He had something to show me. However, on this occasion, I had to look at the natural realm in order to lean into the spirit realm and see what it was that He wanted to reveal to me.

So, I began to look around the auditorium. It was not the first time I had seen in the spirit realm while at church. There have been many occasions that I have seen and partnered with the angelic, seen heavenly items or objects being given out or released, and even heavenly doors open, however this was the first time He was telling me to look with the intention of 'seeing'.

Normally I just look and see, rather than look '*to see*'. This was a major shift and key for me that I now use all the time! The difference here is that when you look '*to see*', you are looking at what is around you in the natural with the intentionality to see through it into what is there in the realm of the spirit. It is like adjusting your eyes to see what is hidden. Remember the pictures that had hidden pictures inside them, like 'Where's Wally'? He is there in the picture, but it takes time to look *to see* where he is hidden. It's often the same concept in the spirit realm.

As I looked around, I was drawn to a young lady in the front row. This young lady had come from a very rough background and had made some pretty poor life choices. However, it seemed that she had gotten her life into some sort of order and was now doing really well.

As I looked at her in the natural, I suddenly SAW! Suddenly it was like my eyes saw beyond the natural and I was looking at what was hidden in the spiritual. I saw a black, fuzzy being attached to her. As I looked at it, Holy Spirit said, 'That is a sexual spirit that has attached itself to her and she is still making choices that are enabling it.'

To anyone else, this young lady seemed to have cleaned up her act. She was worshipping and she had told leaders in her life all the 'right things' however all of a sudden, I was seeing the truth. There were things that she had been keeping hidden.

This was not to condemn or expose her because love always covers, but the kindness of God leads to repentance. He is committed to her wholeness, on every level. When Holy Spirit reveals what's concealed, it opens a door for freedom.

> *To discern is to recognise, be aware of or know something through our senses, by the power of Holy Spirit.*

It is really similar to perception. The main difference being to discern is to use our spiritual senses to judge a person, spirit, atmosphere, or situation accurately. The Bible tells us, in 1 Corinthians 12:8-10, that discernment is primarily a gift about the discerning of spirits.

Another time we were praying and worshipping with friends in our home. Suddenly I saw that every time we interceded for something or someone, a 'package' appeared. They began to stack up and immediately, as I watched, I saw two angels coming and taking turns to collect them, one by one, and dispatch them. These were delivery angels! It was amazing! Every intercessory cry became a tangible answer that was then collected by one of these angels who would pick it up and deliver it swiftly. Our faith rose to another level!

Discernment also helps us to know how to partner with Holy Spirit. It is insight into what is going on in the realm of the spirit. You might see something that the enemy is up to, or you might see something the angels are doing. Either way, once you see, you can partner.

> *But solid food is for the mature, for those who have their powers of discernment trained by constant practice to distinguish good from evil.*
> *Hebrews 5:14 ESV*

Do you see that? Our discernment comes from 'constant' practice and is for the purpose of distinguishing between good and evil. When we 'look to see', we are partnering with Holy Spirit in the gift of discernment.

Our highest use of discernment and our greatest honour is to always discern what God is doing.

Ultimately, it is a gift that Holy Spirit uses to bring people into 'sozo' – salvation, healing and freedom.

ACTIVATE

1. Discerning the Angelic

Discernment of angels doesn't mean we become unhealthy in our awareness of them. We are never called to worship or pray to angels. We aren't even called to order them around or have relationship with them. The purpose of practising to 'see' angels is to sharpen our discernment so that we can see what is happening in the spirit realm. When we discern the angelic, we can partner with them, and the mission Holy Spirit has them on. Likewise, they partner with us too. They are servants of God who live on mission – just like us!

> "Then Jacob awoke from his sleep and said,
> "Surely the LORD is in this place, and I wasn't even aware of it!"
> Genesis 28:16 NLT

We want to train ourselves to become aware of Him and the realm of the spirit, which includes angels.

For those in the Bible, angels were a very real part of their lives. They did not pray to them, order them around or worship them – that would be foolish! But it is equally foolish to completely ignore them.

Angels are beings created by God who not only share his messages, but also actively do his will, encourage believers, and fight spiritual battles on our behalf. The word angel comes from a Greek word that literally means "messenger," and angels are often seen bringing messages from God to us.

In this activation, we are going to practise discerning the presence and ministry of angels.

> *"Are not all the angels ministering spirits sent out [by God]*
> *to serve (accompany, protect) those who will inherit salvation?*
> *[Of course they are!]"*
> Hebrews 1:14 (AMP)

Activation

1. Play some instrumental worship music softly in the background.
2. Focus your love on Jesus. Look for His face.
3. Invite Holy Spirit to come and awaken your senses.
4. Take a deep breath and relax in His love.
5. Now ask that God would send an angel to minister to you. (Hebrews 1:14)
6. Wait, receive, and see or sense what you feel. You may get an impression, or a sense, or a knowing – these are all valid.
7. Where is the angel in the room? What sort of angel is it? Is it big or small? Has the angel got anything in its hands?
8. Now ask Holy Spirit what this angel is here for. Does it have a name? (Sometimes names help clarify the role it has). Does it have something to give you?
9. How can you partner with this angel? Is there something you need to do or release?
10. Take time to centre back in on Jesus and thank Him for this encounter and for His angelic host. Remember, the goal is always Jesus – not the angel. Give Jesus the glory for this time.
11. Journal/write it down or draw a picture of the angel and what its purpose is for.

Groups

1. Leader: Play some instrumental worship music softly in the background.
2. Have everyone get into a comfortable position.
3. Instruct the group as follows:
4. Invite Holy Spirit to come and awaken your senses.
5. Take a deep breath and relax in His love.
6. Now ask that God would send an angel to minister to you. (Please note that we are looking for angels, not the demonic).
7. Wait, receive, and become aware of what you feel. You may get an impression, or a sense, or a knowing – these are all valid.
8. Where is the angel in the room? What sort of angel is it? Is it big or small? Has the angel got anything in its hands?
9. Now ask Holy Spirit what this angel is here for. Does it have a name? (Sometimes names help clarify the role it has). Does it have something to give you?
10. Share with the whole group.
11. Was there anyone who saw/sensed the same angel in the room?
12. If there was more than one that saw a particular angel in the room (e.g., an Angel of Hope or a Scribe Angel), invite people who need or want what that angel has in their lives to stand up and go to the people who 'saw' that angel.
13. Have those people pray and release what the angel has brought into the room over those who want/need that. For example, if someone comes to the person who saw an Angel of Hope, release 'hope' into their lives and situations. If a person comes because of the Scribe Angel, chances are they are in the process of writing or dreaming of writing a book. Pray for a release of anointing to write that is there because of that angel.

> 14. Finish up by taking time to centre back in on Jesus and thank Him for this encounter and for His angelic host. Remember, the goal is always Jesus – not the angel. Give Jesus the glory for this time.

2. Discerning to See

In this activation we are training our eyes to see the realm of the spirit around us.

Please note that we are not looking for the activity of the enemy or the demonic in this particular activation. We are focusing on what God is doing and releasing.

Activation

> 1. Close your eyes and ask Holy Spirit where to look in the room.
> You may sense a specific direction to look towards. You might suddenly picture a place in your mind. You may just get a vague impression towards a certain area.
> If, for whatever reason, you can't get a clear sense of where to look, just pick a spot that catches your attention. It could be a door, behind someone, above us in the room; something on the wall or window …
>
> 2. Open your eyes, look at the spot, and ask Holy Spirit to show you what's there.
> You may see something with your physical eyes.
> Some people see a flash of light or colour; others see a ripple in the atmosphere, like heat off a road on a hot day and for others it might be like a hologram effect.
> If you don't see anything don't be discouraged! Remember that it's by practice that our senses are trained. Try looking for it the same way you would for an answer from Holy Spirit or a prophetic word. A picture may come to your mind, or a sentence. Maybe even an impression or feeling, like joy or peace, which can be an indication of what is in that space. Lean into that.

3. Ask Holy Spirit to explain what you are seeing or sensing. It may only be simple but that is ok! Holy Spirit is always wanting to share this realm with us. This is an important step in the process as it takes us from just 'seeing' for the sake of seeing to learning how to partner with what we are seeing, which is the whole point of the gift of discernment.

4. Now ask Holy Spirit 'why' you are seeing what you are seeing; and what is it there for? Make sure you write down or draw what He tells you.

5. Take time to thank Jesus for this experience and ask Holy Spirit to continue to sensitise your sense of 'seeing' as well as teach you how to partner with what you see.

Groups

1. Leader: lead the whole group through the above activation. Be sure to pace it so that people have time to encounter the realm of the Spirit and the angelic.

2. Have people share what they discerned or saw. If, for example, they sensed or saw an angel in a particular part of the room wanting to release breakthrough or healing, have everyone who needs breakthrough or healing (or whatever it is that they discerned) stand up and go to that spot. This is a prophetic act of faith based on what is in the room right now.

3. Have the person who sensed/saw what was there, partner with it and pray for everyone who has stepped up or in, to receive it.

4. If it's for healing, have them test it out right there and celebrate if they are healed; if its freedom, partner with that and release freedom to those who need it.

5. Come back as a whole group and share some testimonies.

6. Take time to give a shout of praise to Jesus.

3. Discerning Different Atmospheres: Part 1

Activation

1. Play some quiet, instrumental worship music in the background (optional).
2. Get comfortable and tune in your attention and affection to Jesus.
3. Trade tension for attention. This is where you get to deeply breathe His Presence in and release all tension and striving. Tension and stress are blockers to receiving. Let it all go.
4. Invite Holy Spirit to open up your awareness to the realm of the spirit. You might pray something like this: 'Holy Spirit, I give you my soul – my mind, will and emotions. I ask you to awaken my senses to Your presence and to the realm of the spirit. Thank you that You are the Spirit of Revelation. Let every sense I have be on high alert to all you want to reveal to me. In Jesus Name, Amen.'
5. Go for a 1-2 minute walk around your home or the room you are in. Visit some entrances or an area where you spend time with the Lord.
6. Pay attention to how you feel in your emotions, body, and spirit. Can you sense a shift in some of these places? If so, take note of that and what it feels like.
7. Go for another walk for 1-2 minutes to another area.
8. After 1-2 minutes, write down what you sensed or felt and where.
9. Ask Holy Spirit what He wants you to do with what He has shown you.
10. Now partner with that. For example, if you saw a waterfall over the doorway, go and stand in it. If you saw an angel with provision in the corner of the room, go there and thank Jesus for what He has released to you in terms of provision and take it.

Groups

1. Leader: lead the whole group through the above activation. Be sure to pace it so that people have time to encounter Jesus.
2. You may want to play some soaking music softly in the background to help people switch off to distractions and tune into Presence.
3. Have everyone repeat the prayer in Point 4 out loud, all together.
4. Keep following the steps of the activation, giving time for people to walk around the room and discern what is there.
5. After 2 minutes, have people stand or sit where they felt something the strongest or where they feel most drawn to.
6. Leader: Go around the room to where people are standing and ask them to share what they felt or saw.
7. Is there anyone who felt or saw the same thing in that space?
8. Now partner with what has been revealed. Have people pray out loud, releasing what they have discerned. If it's a waterfall, they might pray that everyone encounters the refreshing of the waterfall or the invitation to go deeper. If it's breakthrough, pray to release that. If it's keys, pray for unlocking.
9. Come back together as a group and thank Jesus. Give Him a round of applause!

4. Discerning Atmospheres: Part 2

Activation

1. This activation requires you to go outside. Ask Holy Spirit to help you choose a location that is not too far away from where you are (e.g., a park; a lake; a street corner; a streetlight in your street; etc). If you are unable to go

far then you can go to the front garden. The aim is to be outside of your home and be able to hear and feel in the natural to help you discern the spiritual. If you can't sense 'where', just go out and stand somewhere! Don't over-spiritualise it.

2. When you get to your 'spot' invite Holy Spirit to awaken your senses to the spirit realm.

3. Begin to focus on the natural sounds and feelings you get when you are there. Slow down so that you can 'hear' what is happening around you. Is the wind blowing in the trees? Can you hear birds singing? Is there the sound of water rippling or cars in the distance? Do the same with what you are feeling. Is it warm, or is it cold on your skin? Is there a breeze? Stay a moment in the awareness of what you are feeling in the natural.

4. Now, close your eyes and begin to focus on what you feel or sense in the spirit realm. Ask Holy Spirit to help you tune in to what is happening. You might get an emotion – like fear or overwhelming love; you might get a picture or a sense of something playing out; you might get a word that you see (this could even be triggered by something natural you see, like a street sign or sky writing or a cloud formation).

5. Once you discern something in that place, ask Holy Spirit what He wants you to do with it.

6. Now partner with what He has asked you to do. Do you need to shift the atmosphere? Do you need to release something (like peace or forgiveness?); do you need to prophetically do something, like put a memorial stone down or shake the dust off your feet?
Do whatever He tells you to do.

7. Go back home and journal your experience.

Groups

The aim of this activation is to go outside into a different space to practise discernment.

If outside is not an option, go to other rooms in the house or venue (be sure to spread out and not have everyone in the same location).

Be sure to give them a time limit and an expectation of when to be back.

Have the activation copied out or alternatively have each participant take a photo of it, so that each group has the instructions to follow.

1. Get into pairs or small groups of 3-4 and ask Holy Spirit where He wants your group to go (somewhere in proximity – garden, carpark, street, sidewalk…). Share what the group is feeling with each other and choose where you'll go based on that.

2. If this is possible, have the groups move outside to a park, playground or garden, sidewalk or even a car park or bus stop that is in close proximity to the meeting. A place they felt Holy Spirit leading them to.

3. When groups get to their 'spot', have them invite Holy Spirit and ask Him to awaken their senses to the spirit realm.

4. Begin to focus on the natural sounds and feelings you get when you are there. Slow down so that you can 'hear' what is happening around you. Is the wind blowing in the trees? Can you hear birds singing? Is there the sound of water rippling or cars in the distance? Do the same with what you are feeling. Is it warm, or is it cold on your skin? Is there a breeze? Stay a moment in the awareness of what you are feeling in the natural.

5. Now, close your eyes and begin to focus on what you feel or sense in the spirit realm. Ask Holy Spirit to help you tune in to what is happening. You might get an emotion – like fear or overwhelming love; you might get a picture or a sense of something playing out; you might get a word that you see (this could even be triggered by something natural you see, like a street sign or skywriting).

6. Once you discern something in that place, ask Holy Spirit what He wants you to do with it.

7. Have each share with their small group.

8. Now as a group, partner with what He has asked you to do. Do you need to shift the atmosphere? Do you need to release something (like peace or forgiveness?); do you need to prophetically do something, like put a memorial stone down or shake the dust off your feet? Do whatever He tells you to do.
9. Come back as a whole group and have a representative of each group share their experiences.

5. Discerning in the Nations

Activation

Materials: For this activation you will need a world map or globe.

1. Go to your secret place – a space where you can focus on Jesus and give Him your full attention.
2. Play some soaking music softly in the background.
3. Look at the map/globe and ask Holy Spirit to highlight a nation to you. You might get the name; you might just be drawn to a particular nation.
4. Now ask Holy Spirit to tell you/show you 2 things about this nation:

    - What is God doing in this nation? What is the angelic assignment to see this happen or be released or play-out in that nation?
    - What is the enemy's assignment in this nation? Do you see any particular demonic strongholds or activity at work?

5. Write down what you get/see/sense. You might want to write down your prayer and/or declaration for this nation from what has been revealed to you.
6. Now begin to partner with what Holy Spirit has shown you and pray accordingly for this nation.

7. Finish by standing on or around your map (if you can), or laying hands on it, and take time to praise and worship Jesus over the nations.

Groups

Leader: Put up a world map on the screen.

Materials: Printed world maps to hand out.

Optional: Large world map outline on a drop-sheet or material that is big enough to put onto the floor for the group to stand on or stand around.

1. Have everyone find a space on their own to focus in on Jesus.
2. Play some soaking music softly in the background.
3. Lead the group through the activation above. Be sure to pace it so that everyone has time to encounter and hear/see what is on the heart of the Father for the nation Holy Spirit highlights to them.
4. Make sure they write down the answers to the 2 questions they are to ask Holy Spirit. This is part of training in discernment of spirits.
5. Bring the group back together as a whole and invite people to share the nation they got and the 2 answers to these questions:

    - What is God/the angelic doing in that nation?
    - What is the demonic up to in that nation?

6. Take time to partner with what Holy Spirit has shown and pray for the nations. If the group is large, do this in smaller groups of 3 or 4.
7. Finish by standing on or around the world map and worshipping Jesus over the nations.

CHAPTER 6

Positioned to Perceive

The definition of perception is: the ability to see, hear, or become aware of or conscious of something through the senses or through our mind.

Some synonyms for 'perceive' are to distinguish, feel, grasp, identify, observe, realise, and recognise.

These words help to give us language for how and what we can 'pick up' in the spirit realm.

One day as I was spending time with Jesus in my lounge room, I suddenly became aware of a small child leaning over on the ground next to me. It was so real and unexpected that I quickly opened my eyes, but I was alone in my lounge room. I closed my eyes again and instantly saw this little child, crouched over on the ground. I looked closer and saw that the ground she was on was made up of dry and dusty dirt, and she seemed to be hiding in fear. As my eyes locked in on the child, I began to just 'know' things about this child. I perceived that she was a little girl living in a nation in the Middle East and that she was terrified.

My heart began to break as I began to sense the horrors she most likely had witnessed, atrocities no child should ever have to see or live through. I reached out to touch her but all I felt was air. I felt so broken and helpless. She seemed to become aware of me and looked up with a wide-eyed stare, like a hunted animal. Oh, how I wanted to rescue this little one and hold her safe in my arms. To comfort her and protect her; to take her away from her pain and the terror. Her eyes had seen more horror than I could ever imagine.

Here I was in the comfort of my own home, in one of the safest nations in the world, while this child was all alone, in one of the darkest places on earth. I began to weep as I passionately prayed and spoke words of love, hope and life over this little girl. I began to declare destiny words over her as they leapt into my spirit. My Mumma's heart could not contain the pain and I cried out to the Lord. 'What am I looking at? Why are you showing me this child when I can't do anything for her? Who is she?' I had lots of questions.

Holy Spirit whispered to my heart, 'She is my beloved'. As I began praying again and speaking light and glory into that dark, lonely place I suddenly heard the word 'Aisha' in my spirit. I knew this had to be her name.

I googled the name, and this definition came up: "*She who lives*" or "*Alive and well*".

I suddenly got a sense of a bigger picture. This little girl represented the church in this nation – young, broken, in fear and hiding. The enemy wants nothing more than to wipe her out, but Holy Spirit was declaring 'this is My beloved' and I want you to partner with me and declare over her that 'you are alive and well', that the church in that region would be known as 'she who lives'. This was one of the most profound and powerful times I have ever had in prayer and intercession, and it all happened in my lounge room!

Intimacy with Jesus positions us to perceive.

In his letter to the Ephesians, Paul prays this:

> "*…that the God of our Lord Jesus Christ, the glorious Father, may give you a spirit of wisdom and revelation in your knowledge of Him. <u>I ask that the eyes of your heart may be enlightened, so that you may know the hope of His calling, the riches of His glorious inheritance in the saints,</u> and the surpassing greatness of His power to us who believe. These are in accordance with the working of His mighty strength…*"
> Ephesians 1:17-18 (BSB)

Let's have a closer look at what Paul is talking about here. We don't have 'eyes on our hearts' so what does he mean?

The word for eyes here is **'ophthalmos'** and in this context refers to the 'mind's eye' – in other words, your ability to 'see, hear, and become aware of something through your spiritual senses and imagination'. That is spiritual perception.

The reason your eyes are 'enlightened' or become awakened is so that you may know. Knowing begins with seeing. As you perceive, you see and then you know. That is really important to grasp. Perceiving is a way of seeing, hearing and sensing that leads to knowing.

That's radical right there! In other words, our ability to know all that Paul mentions in Ephesians 1:17-18, is fundamentally connected to our ability to perceive. The eyes of our hearts are opened *so that we can know…*

The word enlightened here is not weirdly mystical or something to be afraid of. Before the devil broadcasted his version of this word, it was already God's. It simply means to light up and illuminate.

We can't *know* anything without Holy Spirit shining His light upon our hearts and minds and opening our spiritual senses. There is a whole realm of glory that we are invited to come and encounter!

His very word is a lamp to our feet and a light to our path. (Psalm 119:105)

The genesis of the world began with a declaration: *"Let there be light…"* from Light Himself. (Genesis 1:3) Jesus, Light of the world. (John 8:12)

Holy Spirit is the Spirit of Wisdom and of Revelation – it's what He does. He reveals!

Paul wouldn't pray a prayer that was never available or achievable let alone permissible. It wasn't just a nice prayer or religious terminology of the day. He had an expectation, based on his own experience, that believers would have the 'eyes of their heart' opened to encounter all that was within reach to them.

As Jesus often said, "… the Kingdom of heaven is at hand." (Matthew 10:7 NKJV)

That means it's within reach. Whose hand is it at? Yours and mine!

Remember that we go from *glory to glory.* (2 Corinthians 3:18) That also includes what we experience. Our experiences should be from glory to glory!

Paul knew of these encounters first-hand. They were a normal part of his life. Listen to what he says:

> *"I must go on boasting. Although there is nothing to gain,*
> *I will go on to visions and revelations from the Lord.*
> *I know a man in Christ who fourteen years ago was caught up to*
> *the third heaven. Whether it was in the body or out of it I do not*
> *know, but God knows. And I know that this man—whether in*
> *the body or out of it I do not know, but God knows…"*
> *2 Corinthians 12:2 (NIV)*

Paul did not know whether what he experienced was *in the body or out of the body.* That tells us that both are completely plausible, acceptable, and available. All he knew was that he had an incredible heavenly encounter.

On the Isle of Patmos, John had a series of revelatory encounters. These were supernatural and John was invited to 'come up here and see...'

> *"After this I looked and saw a door standing open in heaven.*
> *And the voice I had previously heard speak to me*
> *like a trumpet was saying, "Come up here, and I will show you*
> *what must happen after these things."*
> *At once I was in the Spirit, and I saw a throne standing*
> *in heaven, with someone seated on it...."*
> Revelation 4:1 (BSB)

This was a clear invitation for John to encounter the kingdom of God and that meant so much more than head-knowledge or theology. This was to be a radical encounter of heaven!

Can you see that encounters are part of the normal Christian life?

Holy Spirit wants you to be positioned so that you may perceive all that He wants you to partner with. Why? So that you can see, and then release, on earth as it is in heaven!

ACTIVATE

1. What is Your Fragrance?

Activation

> 1. Go to your secret place and shut the door. Matthew 6:6 says that the Father is there waiting for you.

2. Ask Holy Spirit: What is my fragrance? You might see a beautiful bottle; or a colour; or you might smell a fragrance or have a thought come to mind, for example jasmine or vanilla. Write down or draw what it looks like and/or smells like.
3. Ask Holy Spirit: What is the name of my fragrance? Can you see the name on the bottle?
4. Now ask Him: What is the purpose of it? For example, if it is lavender, it's purpose may be to release peace and rest.
5. Holy Spirit wants to put that fragrance on you right now! Allow Him to do that!
6. How does your 'fragrance' speak to your identity and mission?
7. Is there a way you can release the fragrance you've been given today to those around you?

Groups

1. Play some instrumental worship music softly in the background.
2. Leader: take everyone through the above steps in the activation. Be sure to pace it so that people have time to encounter and engage.
3. Allow time for everyone to write down/draw their fragrance and answer the questions around identity and mission.
4. Depending on the size of your group, you can have each person come and share what they received and then release that over everyone OR break up into smaller groups of 2-4 and do the same.

2. What Am I Dressed In?

Activation

1. Spend a moment inviting the Presence of Holy Spirit.
2. Ask Him to show you an 'outfit' He has dressed you in (e.g., it may be a deep-sea diving suit or a ball gown).
3. What does your outfit look like? Write down what you see or draw a picture.
4. Holy Spirit loves questions, so ask Him some more questions about the outfit and the details you see. Why that colour? Why that outfit? Is there a number, word, picture, or symbol on what He has given you? What does it mean?
5. Continue to journal all that He shows you.
6. Is this outfit for the season you are currently in or the season you are going into?
7. Spend time thanking Him for it.
8. Outreach: Next time you are at church or with a family member or friend, ask Holy Spirit to show you an outfit He has for one of them.
9. Write it down or draw it, then share that with them. Make sure it is encouraging, uplifting, and edifying.

Groups

1. Leader: Get everyone into pairs.
2. Lead the group through the above activation steps, however, tell them that each person has to ask Holy Spirit to show them an outfit for their partner. Ask this question: 'What is my partner dressed in and why?'
3. Look at the details. What colour is it? What type of outfit is it? (e.g., is it a uniform or a ball gown etc.)
4. Take a few minutes to write or draw what you see. If you draw it, be sure to put labels on it.

5. Is there something your partner needs to 'take off' in order to put on the new?
6. Take time to share with each other.
7. If they need to remove something, now is the time to pray with them to see that item come off.
8. Now bless your partner with the new outfit. Give it to them and invite Holy Spirit to 'fit' it to them and activate what it is for in their lives.

3. Step into your new shoes

> *"...Keep in step with the Spirit."*
> *Galatians 5:25 (NIV)*

Activation

1. Quiet yourself down and invite Holy Spirit to breathe on you and awaken your senses to His Presence and the spirit realm.
2. In your imagination space, I want you to see Jesus. He is giving you new shoes to put on.
3. What do these shoes look like? What style are they? What colour? Do they have anything on them (symbols/writing etc?)
4. Now ask Jesus: 'Why these shoes?' 'What are these shoes for in this season of my life or for the season that is coming?'
5. As a prophetic act, put these shoes on and walk around your room or house. In a sense, you are prophetically wearing them in! Begin to declare out loud what He has said about the purpose of these shoes. Step into your destiny.
6. Ask Holy Spirit what He wants you to do right now. For example, if you were given 'gum boots', He might want you

to jump in spiritual puddles! If you were given 'sneakers/runners', He may want you to run! By faith, do what He tells you to do!

7. Be sure to write down or draw what Holy Spirit has shown you in this activation.

Groups

1. Follow the same activation instructions as above. Have a leader read them out and be sure to pace it so that people get to engage and encounter Jesus in this activation.

2. However, in the group activation, each person is receiving a pair of shoes to give away to someone else. The leader will say '…. I want you to see Jesus and He is giving you a pair of new shoes that will be for someone else…' Don't worry about who they're for just yet.

3. Follow the instructions in the activation up to (and including) point number 4 and then stop there.

4. Ask Holy Spirit what He wants the person receiving the shoes to prophetically 'do' once they receive their shoes. If they are 'gum boots', He might want them to jump in spiritual puddles! If they are 'sneakers/runners', He may want them to run!

5. Be sure to have everyone write down/draw everything they see/sense/get so that they can share it with someone in detail.

6. When time is up, have everyone find a partner.

7. Share with each other what shoes Jesus has given you to give away.

8. Now have them 'do' the prophetic act that Jesus told them to do! This is partnering in child-like faith and activating the prophetic.

9. Finish by praying for each other and blessing one another.

4. The Lion's Roar!

Activation

1. Connect in with Jesus and invite Holy Spirit. Welcome His Presence into your space; 'I declare ears to hear and eyes to see what heaven has for you today!'
2. One of the Names of Jesus is the Lion of the Tribe of Judah!
3. Take a moment to see Him as the Lion. You can look with your imagination or sense His Presence standing near you. Look at His majestic form. Look in His eyes. What do you see and what do you sense as He stands there, poised before you as the Lion?
4. He may come close to you. Can you smell Him or feel the warmth of His breath on you?
5. How does it make you feel to be near Him? Do you come close, or do you bow down in reverential awe?
6. Take time to stay in that moment with Him and encounter Him.
7. Now when you're ready, ask: 'Jesus, what do you want to ROAR over me today?' (You may get words, feel His breath, hear a song … be open to the creative way He is speaking to you.)
8. Write down/draw what He tells/shows you.
9. Now ask Him this: What IMPOSSIBILITY in my life do you want to ROAR over?
10. Write down/draw this.
11. Spend time thanking Him for roaring His power, life, solution, provision, and strategy into your impossibility.

Groups

1. Take the group through the above activation. Be sure to pace it so that people get the most out of this encounter.

> 2. After people have had Jesus roar over their own personal impossibilities, have them take it a step further and ask Him: 'What impossibility would you like to roar over that is in my city/nation or the nations right now?' (It might be the suicide rates; or homelessness or it might be a war that is going on; etc.)
> 3. Write down/draw what He shows you.
> 4. Have people come up and share what they got for their city/nation/nations and then pray in line with that 'roar' to see that impossibility shift.
> 5. When the whole group is done, play a victory song that you can all sing together because of what the Lion of Judah has roared over every impossibility.

5. Who are you for me today, Jesus?

> *'... man shall not live on bread alone*
> *but by every word that comes from the mouth of God.'*
> *Matthew 4:4 (BSB)*

God is speaking 'now' words that are life to us! These are His 'Rhema' words. These are His *spoken* words, and He is speaking presently and continually. Today we are going to lean in and listen to what He is saying.

Activation

> 1. Quiet yourself before the Lord and lean in close. Get into a place of rest because it's in that place that you are going to be able to perceive and receive all that He wants to tell you and/or give you.
> 2. Ask Jesus: 'Who do you want to be for me today?' It could be that He wants to be your deliverer; your 'very great reward'; your Prince of Peace; your Champion… (Let Holy Spirit speak and reveal it to you).
> 3. Now ask: 'What do you want to do in me today?' Be sure to

write down/draw what He says in your journal.

4. Now ask Him: 'What do you want to do through me today?' (This may be a prophetic act or declaration. He may ask you to contact someone or to go somewhere and release something …Be open and ready.)

5. Journal and then do what He tells you to do!

Groups

1. Play some instrumental worship music softly in the background.

2. Leader: Read out the above activation steps with the group. Remember to pace it so that everyone has time to enter into the encounter.

3. Bring the group back as a whole and invite 2 or 3 to share their experience.

4. When they get to the part about what Jesus wants to do 'through' them, there may be an invitation for others in the group to respond here as well. The leader will have to facilitate this. For example, if someone says that Jesus wants to heal through them, invite those that need healing to stand and have that person pray for them. If someone says that Jesus wants them to reconcile with a family member, invite all those that need reconciliation to stand and have that person pray…etc.

CHAPTER 7

Positioned in Expectation

There are many times in the Bible where God speaks through very natural objects and circumstances. Jesus also did the same, as too does Holy Spirit. Why? Because at the core of it, the heart of God is to connect with His people, and He has many ways He does that.

God is always looking to speak to us. As we live intentionally aware of His Presence and on mission, we become attuned to His voice breaking into our (mostly) very normal days!

I cannot tell you the number of times that Holy Spirit has grabbed my attention and spoken to me through number plates as I am driving! Here I am going about my very normal day, doing school drop-offs, and going to work and, suddenly, a car in front of me has a number plate that grabs my attention!

Just the other day I was behind a number plate that said Acts 7:33. That scripture says: "Then the LORD said to him, 'Take off your sandals, for you are standing on holy ground.'" (NIV) Can you believe it? That number plate was an invitation to me by Holy Spirit to be aware of His interruption, come close and step onto holy ground. A modern-day burning bush you might say!

Another time a number plate in front of me grabbed my attention because it said 'Harvest'. Well, it actually said 'HRVEST', but my mind instantly read the word 'Harvest'. I immediately began praying for the harvest and in line with Matthew 9:38 which says, *"so pray to the Lord who is in charge of the harvest; ask him to send more workers into his fields."* (NLT) As I was praying, within seconds another car literally went in front of me with the word 'saved' and then another with the word 'saved' again. I know, it sounds crazy right?

Later that night someone came by to see me unexpectedly, with her boyfriend, and they both ended up giving their lives to the Lord!

How amazing is it when we become aware of God breaking into our ordinary lives and partner with His heart and mission?

One more story! We were on a mission trip in the Philippines and this particular day we were doing a treasure hunt. A 'treasure hunt' is where Holy Spirit gives you clues to look for as you go on outreach. As we were praying, I looked out and my eyes were drawn to a vibrant, hot-pink flower. As I looked at that flower, I saw in my mind, a young girl with long black hair. I instantly knew in my spirit that Holy Spirit was going to lead me to a young girl with long black hair, who was going to be wearing a bright, hot-pink t-shirt.

Most of the afternoon we didn't see this 'treasure' with the long black hair and hot-pink t-shirt. Just as we were getting ready to go back, I suddenly saw her! There in the park was a young girl with long black hair and a hot-pink t-shirt on. We approached her and I introduced myself and explained that God had spoken to me in the morning about her. She was shocked! As I shared the love of Jesus and the Gospel with her, tears welled up and she gave her life to Him. That hot-pink flower was the very thing that led to the salvation of a precious young girl!

What a joy to partner with Holy Spirit!

It is Holy Spirit who searches the depths of the Father and then reveals it to us! (1 Corinthians 2:10). There are so many ways that He does this and one of them is through using very natural objects. Why? Because we understand the 'natural' and He will use what we know to reveal the mysteries of the Kingdom and His heart to us.

When we practise partnering with Him in this way, whether it be at home, or in places like school or church or even our car, we're learning to be attentive and open to hearing Holy Spirit speak in our everywhere, and in everything. He is our Teacher. He is the Spirit of revelation. That's whose voice we are leaning in to hear and becoming attuned to.

Remember that the goal is to have our senses trained. We start to become intentionally aware and expectant that God wants to speak to us in our everyday and everywhere.

The reality is that there are objects all around us and any one of them may be the catalyst for God speaking specifically into a situation in our own lives or the lives of others.

Of course, there are many, many ways God speaks to us, and this is just one of them.

Let's look at some examples in Scripture and let's begin by having a look at Exodus 3:1-4 (ESV)

> *"One day Moses was tending the flock of his father-in-law, Jethro, the priest of Midian. He led the flock far into the wilderness and came to Sinai, the mountain of God. There the angel of the Lord appeared to him in a blazing fire from the middle of a bush. Moses stared in amazement. Though the bush was engulfed in flames, it didn't burn up. "This is amazing," Moses said to himself. "Why isn't that bush burning up? I must go see it." When the Lord saw Moses coming to take a closer look, God called to him from the middle of the bush, "Moses! Moses!" "Here I am!" Moses replied."*

Here we see that God was using something very natural to grab Moses' attention. A burning bush wasn't anything particularly out of the ordinary, however what was strange with this burning bush was, although the bush was on fire, it wasn't burning up! This was enough to stir up Moses' curiosity to come and take a closer look.

Could it be that at times, God is setting up unusual circumstances or distractions in the natural world, I like to call them *supernatural diversions*, to see if we will come near?

We see that it was in the 'coming near' that the Lord then spoke to Moses. Moses didn't have an initial thought that this burning bush could be a God set up. He was just fascinated and came close!

This is why God loves to speak through very ordinary and natural things. He loves to see if we will lean in or come closer and it's only then that He will speak. He is trying to grab our attention. Will we come close?

Let's have another look into the Old Testament, in the book of Jeremiah.

> *"And the word of the LORD came to me, asking, "What do you see, Jeremiah?" "I see a branch of an almond tree," I replied. "You have observed correctly," said the LORD, "for I am watching over My word to accomplish it."*
> Jeremiah 1:11 (BSB)

Jeremiah looked and saw what was quite possibly in his line of view, a branch of an almond tree. You can't get more natural than that! When he told God what He saw, God then gave a prophetic word.

You see, the prophetic was released when Jeremiah said what he 'saw', even if it was purely natural.

The natural is often the catalyst for the supernatural!

Time and time again we read that God used objects and strange methods and/or actions to bring about the prophetic word, for healing, to reveal truth, to speak prophetic warnings, and, of course, to show His Presence.

Abraham was asked to look at the stars in the sky and the grains of sand and when He did, God spoke about his prophetic destiny as a Father to the nations.

The list goes on and on!

When Jesus walked on earth, He most often spoke in parables which can be described as *'earthly stories with heavenly meanings'*. These stories were based on natural things.

Jesus also did this when He told the disciples they only had to have faith the size of a … what? That's right, the size of a mustard seed! He used something very natural (a mustard seed) to talk about something spiritual – faith. The visual aid of a mustard seed brought an impactful picture that helped explain something that would otherwise be very abstract to the natural mind.

How kind of Jesus to do that. The seed wasn't supernatural, and the seed didn't bring the revelation. It was used by Jesus to demonstrate a spiritual and powerful truth. Jesus wanted people to really get this!

What about in Matthew 22:17-22 when Jesus says to those aiming to trick him, "show me a coin …" Obviously they were talking about taxes, so Jesus used their own currency – a simple coin – to speak about a spiritual reality.

In Acts 21, we see a very clear use of an object, namely a belt, to bring a strong prophetic word. Have a read:

> *"After we had been there several days, a prophet named Agabus came down from Judea. Coming over to us, he took Paul's belt, bound his own feet and hands, and said, "The Holy Spirit says: 'In this way the Jews of Jerusalem will bind the owner of this belt and hand him over to the Gentiles. When we heard this, we and the people there pleaded with Paul not to go up to Jerusalem …."*
> Acts 21:10-12 (BSB)

Imagine that? A prophet taking your belt off you and using it to speak a prophetic word! How did Agabus know to do that? The belt wasn't anointed or revelatory, but it was a perfect object to demonstrate what was going to happen prophetically. Agabus could have just used words. However, God has a history of using natural objects and actions to reveal spiritual truths and prophetic messages to and through people.

One of the best ways to grow in connecting to, responding to, and moving in the realm of the spirit, is to become like a little child. Let's not let our intellectual minds get in the way.

God uses the foolish things to confound the wise, or some versions say to shame the wise! (See 1 Corinthians 1:27) Oh how true this can be!

The late John Wimber of the Vineyard movement said it like this: "God offends the mind, to reveal the heart".

Let's not allow offence or intellectualism to be the blockers to our encounters with God. Instead, let's have an expectation that God is wanting to speak to us, and may very well be trying to speak through the very natural things around us.

Let's be like Moses and 'draw near' so that we are positioned in expectation to hear what the Lord wants to say and release.

ACTIVATE

1. What's Behind the Door?

As I spent time with Jesus, I saw a picture of a long hallway, much like when you're staying in a hotel. I had this sense that He was inviting us to walk down the hallway and find our 'door'. There is a heavenly 'door' that is waiting for you to walk through! What is on the other side of your 'door'? I believe that for some it will be a fresh encounter with Jesus. For others it will be the next 'mission' or 'assignment' that He has for you to step into. For some others of you it will be a time of refreshing and restoring.

The significance of walking through doors represents stepping into what God has for you. Your door and what's behind it is unique and created just for you!

Activation

1. Find a quiet place to be with Jesus. Quiet your mind down, open your heart and invite Holy Spirit to come.
2. In your imagination space, picture yourself in the hallway. Walk down that hallway and choose a door.
3. What does the door look like? Is there a number on it? Remember, God is in the details!
4. Open the door and walk in! What is in there? Is it a room or is it a garden or something else? The options are limitless!
5. What do you see there? Is Jesus there?
6. What does this mean for you and the season you're in right now?

Groups

1. Leader: lead the whole group through the above activation. Be sure to pace it so that people have time to encounter Jesus.

2. You may want to play some soaking music softly in the background to help people switch off to distractions and tune into Presence.

3. Once the activation is done, have people share in small groups of 3 or 4 and release what Jesus has shown them to the others in their group.

2. Everyday Superheroes!

Jesus is the hero of this life-story, and he is better than any made up superhero!

Just like superheroes, we too are called and equipped to live supernatural lives with the supernatural power of Holy Spirit.

Superheroes have names and costumes that define and identify them.

Most of the time we see what's on the outside when we look or think of ourselves and think it's just 'little ole me' without letting God define us. He wants to take off the layers that restrict, label, and squeeze our lives into something that isn't His truth.

He wants us to see what *He sees* and live out of that – our Holy Spirit SUPER-natural identity!

Activation

1. Go to your secret place and take a moment to focus your heart's attention on Jesus. Invite Holy Spirit to increase your awareness of Him and the supernatural realm that is all around you.

2. Now ask Holy Spirit to show you how God the Father sees you?

3. What has He given you that makes you supernaturally YOU?

4. Ask Holy Spirit: If I had a heavenly superhero costume, what would it look like? What colour is it? What powers do I have? What is in my hands (e.g., sword? bow and arrow?) Is there anything on my head? Etc.

5. Ask Him: What is the purpose of my superpower?

6. Now, see yourself take off your 'normal' clothes to reveal the superhero costume that is already on you and part of you! You may even want to do a physical action here. (If Holy Spirit reveals details about what those normal clothes represent, verbalise that as you are removing them. For example, if jacket = intimidation, you could say "I take off intimidation in Jesus' Name…"

7. Make a thankful declaration about who you are according to the heart of God.
Write out your identity declaration like this (this is mine as an example for you):
"I declare Gabby (you insert your name here when you do yours) is a supernatural Wonder Woman. She releases the awe and wonder of heaven everywhere she goes!"

8. Be sure to write down or draw, as well as date what you got in this activation, so you never forget your true identity!

Groups

1. Leader: lead the whole group through the above activation. Be sure to pace it so that people have time to encounter Jesus.

2. You may want to play some soaking music softly in the background to help people switch off to distractions and tune into Presence.

3. Be sure to have everyone take time to write out their identity declaration like this (this is mine):
"I declare Gabby (insert your own name here when you do yours) is a supernatural Wonder Woman! She releases the awe and wonder of heaven everywhere she goes!"

4. Go around the group and have people share their declarations. There is power in saying these out loud. Be sure to celebrate people as they do!

> 5. Now have everyone in the group get up in the space and walk around. As they do that, have them ask Holy Spirit to highlight someone and ask Him what their 'superhero' costume is. (It can be different to what they got for themselves).
> 6. When you see something for someone, stop them and share it with them. You may need them to remove the 'old' identity and then prophetically put on their new identity. They may need to action something. Follow Holy Spirit's lead on this.
> 7. Everyone should be ministering to someone.
> 8. Have the group come back and have 2 or 3 share their experiences.

3. Lean Back

> *"The Lord is my best friend and my shepherd. I always have more than enough. He offers a resting place for me in his luxurious love. His tracks take me to an oasis of peace, the quiet brook of bliss. That's where he restores and revives my life …"*
> *Psalm 23:1-3 (TPT)*

I have such a strong sense that the Father wants to encounter you and love on you right now where you are at.

There is a lot of pressure and weariness in the days we live in, and He is wanting us to 'stop' and come and just 'be' with Him. It is in His Presence, in His arms, heads reclined upon His chest, listening to the rhythm of His heartbeat, that He restores and revives our soul.

So, the invitation is to stop what you're doing and come!

Activation

> 1. Find a space/place that you can sit with the Father. Imagine sitting close to Him. Snuggle up if you can. Rest into Him.

2. Find a song that speaks about resting in His Love and Presence (this one could have words or be instrumental).
3. Take some deep breaths and focus on Jesus. Slow down the busyness and shut off the distractions.
4. What do you feel in this place? What is the Father saying to you?
5. Ask Him what lies you have believed about yourself that He wants to break off. What do you need to do to remove the lie and replace it with His Truth? Let His love overwhelm you. You are safe.
6. Write down what comes to mind in your journal.
7. Now ask the Father: "What is on Your heart that you want to replace that lie with?"
8. You are going to tear up the lies. As a prophetic act, tear up the piece of paper that you wrote the 'lies' on.
9. Now, take a moment to write down the truth that the Father spoke to you.
10. Hold up your piece of paper with the Father's heart/truth and repeat this prayer out loud:
    "Father, thank you for revealing your heart for me. Thank you for breaking the lies that I have lived under. They are no longer my identity. I take this/these truth/s and declare that I will live under the banner of One. I will live under the approval of my Father. I will live from the identity that you have given me. Today/tonight is a new day/night! Amen!"

Groups

1. Make sure everyone has a piece of paper and pen/s.
2. Leader: lead the whole group through the above activation. It is best to explain what is expected of them beforehand; you might even put up the steps on a screen for everyone to refer to.

3. For this activation you are going to play a worship song (look for those that speak about His Presence and Love). This song is to help people switch off to distractions and tune into Presence and begin to 'rest' in the encounter of the Father's love.

4. This is an activation that is personal – between the person and Jesus. They need time to be with Him.

5. When they have had time with Jesus dealing with the lies, have everyone write down their lies on their paper.

6. We are going to tear up the lies. Have everyone break the lies by the prophetic act of tearing up their pieces of paper.

7. Now, take a moment to write down the truth that the Father spoke to you.

8. Have everyone lift up their pieces of paper with the Father's heart/truth on them and have them repeat this after you:

9. "Father, thank you for revealing your heart for me. Thank you for breaking the lies that I have lived under. They are no longer my identity. I take this/these truth/s and declare that I will live under the banner of One. I will live under the approval of my Father. I will live from the identity that you have given me. Today/tonight is a new day/night! Amen!"

4. Change of Season!

With every change of season comes expectation and preparation. We begin to get 'ready' for what is coming ahead. If we're shifting into Autumn, we might get out the beanies or add more blankets to the bed and wear warm slippers! Wood is stacked, ready to light the fire for the cold evenings that are coming.

When we are shifting into Spring, we are taking off blankets, opening windows, the bare trees begin to blossom, and jumpers are replaced with t-shirts as the weather warms up.

You might live somewhere that is tropical and you have a dry and rainy season. There are things you need to do to be 'ready' for the season you find yourself in.

The Bible tells us that there is a time and season for everything under heaven. (Ecclesiastes 3)

Just as in the natural, we have seasons in the spiritual, and that is what we are looking at in our activation today!

Activation

1. Sit with Jesus in your secret place Matthew 6:6.
2. Jesus is inviting you to come with an expectation that He wants to prepare you for this new season.
3. Ask Him these questions:

   - What is it that I need to 'take off' for this new season?
   - Are there areas in my life where the 'windows' were closed but now you want me to open them?
   - Or do I need to 'shut' up some doors and windows?
   - What is it that you want to give me to 'put on' or 'pick up' in this new season?

4. Look at the details (item, colour, any emblems/words, etc.) and ask Him why. Those details are there for a reason and a purpose.
5. Write down or draw what He has shown you in this special time together.

Groups

1. Leader: lead the whole group through the above activation. Be sure to pace it so that people have time to encounter Jesus.
2. You may want to play some soaking music softly in the background to help people switch off to distractions and tune into Presence.
3. Tell them that what Holy Spirit shows them and gives them, is actually going to be for someone else. They don't need to know who yet.

> 4. Have people come up to share the season change and what Jesus has given them to pick up or put on. However, this time they are to release it to someone else in the group.
>
> 5. Now, have them look and see who Holy Spirit is identifying or highlighting. Encourage them to be brave and take a risk!
>
> 6. Have them invite that person to stand and ask them if anything about what you shared resonates with them. If so, release what Holy Spirit gave you over that person. If not, that is ok too! Release a blessing over them.
>
> 7. If this happens, the Leader can ask the whole group who resonated with that season and word. Have these ones stand and receive.

It's important to stretch and take risks so that we grow, even if we miss it or get it wrong. That is why the activation asks for the person to share it with an individual first before asking the whole group.

5. God is Greater!

> *"There is none like You, O Lord;*
> *You are great, and great is Your name in might."*
> *Jeremiah 10:6 (ESV)*

Did you know that God is greater? He alone is the 'Great I Am.'

He is greater than your past, your present and your future. He is right in the middle of your mess, your pain, and your impossibilities. He is even greater than your biggest mistakes on your worst day. He is the Great I Am!

Don't forget that He turned water into wine, ashes to beauty, brokenness to wholeness, hopelessness to greatness, death to life. He is a miracle-working God! He is greater than all the unseen things and powers of darkness that have brought you pain, confusion, torment, and tears.

He is the Great I Am!

And He declares, "I am Greater!"

He is greater than sickness, death, destruction, hell, and demonic spirits.
He is greater than your weakness and the mistakes you have made.
He is greater than your history and your regrets.
He is greater than your circumstances or those that are around you,
He is the Great I Am!

Activation

1. Get into a quiet spot with Holy Spirit.
2. What circumstances in your life have held you down to where you feel like you can't get back up again? Write it/them down on paper.
3. Look at each one and say out loud: "God is GREATER than…"
4. Do something prophetic to release the Truth of that statement. For example, you might feel to jump on that piece of paper; dance over it; tear or scrunch it up or even burn it.
5. Ask Holy Spirit what He wants to fill you with right NOW! It could be fresh joy; it could be fresh courage; it could be fresh ideas!

Groups

For this group activation, you will need to have butcher paper (or large pieces of poster style paper) and colour markers.

Depending on the size of your group, this activation can be done as a whole group or in smaller groups of around 5-10 maximum.

1. Read out the above 'God is Greater' declaration to the whole group.
2. Ask them: "What circumstances in your life have held you down to where you feel like you can't get back up?"
3. Invite Holy Spirit to highlight what is hidden that He wants to heal.

4. The group can begin to share and, as they do, write down their circumstances or things that have held them down in 1 or 2 words. For example: Disappointment; Fear of failure; Rejection; etc.

5. When the group is ready, have them stand on that paper all together and begin to pray together against all the things that have held them back and make a declaration of 'No more!' and 'Freedom'.

6. Now invite Holy Spirit to reveal what He wants to fill each person with right now.

7. Have people in the group share what He shows/tells them and then pray to release it over their group. It might be fresh joy; it might be fresh courage; it might be fresh ideas!

CHAPTER 8

Positioned in Heavenly Places

As I was spending time with Jesus one particular morning, I was feeling completely overwhelmed by the busyness of my life. Everything in the natural realm was clamouring for my attention and I was struggling to focus.

As I cried out 'Help!', Holy Spirit said, 'Come up here!' Immediately I felt myself go 'up' and there I saw some wooden double doors. I felt all the 'stuff' that was trying to pull me and overwhelm me, had followed me there, but as I walked through the doors, they shut, and everything that was harassing me was locked out. I could see the doors bulging as the things from my life pushed against the doors with a life-force of their own, but they couldn't get in!

I found myself in what looked like a lovely little chapel. An instant peace filled me, and I took a deep breath. Suddenly I felt clarity and an energy I didn't have before.

The little chapel was small and quaint with wooden pews. Up the front was a beautiful, stained-glass window. There was something physically tangible and all-encompassing about the peace and the silence of the chapel. No-one else was there. I made my way to the second row from the front and sat down. I wondered if Jesus was going to join me.

Suddenly, the atmosphere became charged, and I became acutely aware of every particle in the room. I knew it was Him! There was no 'Person', however His very being filled the atmosphere itself. It literally became the very air that I breathed! I knew I was in a sacred space, in a heavenly place, and it was one of my most beautiful encounters.

I hope by now you are beginning to realise we have access to heavenly places and spaces.

The Bible tells us that we are seated with Christ in heavenly places.

Colossians 3:2 says "Set your minds on things above and not on things on earth …" Another way to put it is to *fix your mind or anchor your mind on things above.*

In other words, you have a choice where you are going to 'set' or 'fix' your mind.

Anchor your mind onto the things of heaven because that is your identity and perspective. This should be your normal. You get to do this but it's up to you to choose to do this, continually.

You and I are called to be so heavenly minded that we are of absolute earthly good! This is how we become those that release on earth as it is in heaven.

How can we release what we haven't seen or experienced?

Right before Stephen was martyred, we read that he *fixed his gaze into heaven.*

> "But Stephen, full of the Holy Spirit, gazed steadily into heaven and saw the glory of God, and he saw Jesus standing in the place of honour at God's right hand."
> Acts 7:55 NLT

Stephen chose to look into a different realm.

He chose to gaze steadily; to fix his vision; to be fixated and anchored in heaven. When he did, he saw! He saw the glory of God and he saw Jesus. Wow!

When we choose to look into the realm of the Kingdom and fix our gaze there, in other words, anchoring our sight and soul in heaven, we get to SEE Him and that changes everything.

When we see Him, we become like Him.

When we see Him, suddenly His will and His agenda are all that matter.

When we see Him, we can stand firm, unwavering in faith and grace; ready to endure whatever comes our way.

When we see Him, we can partner with heaven.

Come and behold Him! As you see Him and let your gaze linger on Him, He will captivate your heart, again and again and again…

ACTIVATE

1. Intimacy is The Doorway to Heaven

I had an encounter where I was taken into a vision of a heavenly room. In this room I saw Jesus at one end, standing with His arms outstretched. He was shining with brilliant white and coloured light. I ran to embrace Him and as I came in for the hug, He became a double door, opened wide. And Holy Spirit whispered in my heart, "It's in intimacy, as we draw close to the heart of Jesus, that He becomes the access point of heaven and all of heaven's resources."

I was overwhelmed and wowed!

What do you see when you look into the open door of heaven that God wants you to release over your family? What about over your city? How about your nation? Revival is birthed in prayer and through the prophetic declarations of God's people!

Activation

1. Take a moment to focus your attention and look for Jesus. Where is He? Come close to Jesus. You may want to embrace Him as He opens His arms to you.
2. See the double-door of heaven wide open. What is there specifically behind the doors for you to take and release over your family, over your city and over your nation? (it can be word/s; picture; scripture; etc.)
3. Write down or draw what you see/get and then make a declaration over your:
a/ family; b/ city; & c/ nation.
The Bible tells us to declare the things that are not (yet) as though they were. (Romans 4:17)
4. Speak out the prophetic declarations and partner with what you have seen to see revival come.

Groups

Put a picture of double-doors up on the screen as a visual prompt to set the scene. Play some quiet, soaking/instrumental music in the background.

1. Leader: Read out the following steps.

2. Take a moment to focus your attention and look for Jesus. Where is He? Come close to Jesus. You may want to embrace Him as He opens His arms to you.

3. See the heavenly double-door wide open. What is there specifically behind the doors for you to take and release over your family, over your city and over your nation? (it can be word/s; picture/s; scripture/s; etc.)

4. Write down or draw what you see/get and then make a declaration over your:
a/ family; b/ city; & c/ nation.
The Bible tells us to declare the things that are not (yet) as though they were. (Romans 4:17)

5. Create a prayer that partners with what you have seen.

6. Have a couple of people share and pray out their crafted prayer.

7. Finally, have everyone pair up and share and pray together. There is power in our agreement. Let's join with heaven to see revival come.

2. Come Up Higher!

During the week I became super aware of the airwaves around me. They were busy and full of clatter, noise, distractions, and distortion. The message on these airwaves were releasing fear, hopelessness, panic, disillusionment, anxiety, and dread. I felt Holy Spirit say, "Come up higher!" So, I pushed through and went to a heavenly place where the Father was. It was so peaceful and there was such clarity! He then asked me, "What is the message that you are broadcasting over the airwaves?" Heaven has broadcasts to release but we need to 'come up higher' to see and hear them so that we can partner with heaven and release them on earth.

Activation

1. There is an invitation to 'come up higher' today! Take a moment in your secret place to ask Holy Spirit to take you higher – in other words, take you outside of the earthly realm and into the heavenly realm where Jesus and the Father reside.
2. What can you see/hear/feel in this place?
3. What does the Father want you to broadcast on earth? Take a moment to see/hear/feel/sense what He is revealing to you that is being broadcast in heaven.
4. Your words partnered with heaven are powerful! They create, shift, release, pull down, build up and break off!
5. Write down/draw all that Holy Spirit shows you.

Groups

1. Leader: play some soaking music in the background to set the atmosphere.
2. Lead people through the activation steps.
3. Be sure to have them write down or draw what they see/feel/sense/hear.
4. Have everyone share their broadcasts, reminding them that their declarations are as powerful in their mouths as they are in God's.

3. Heaven's Library

Did you know that there are books in heaven?

I had an encounter with Holy Spirit where He took me to a heavenly room and opened a book before me. As I looked at the pages that were open, fascinated, it suddenly dawned on me that this was one of 'my' books in heaven! This was part of 'my' story that was being written and formed. The words on the pages were alive and moving and flashing in wispy, golden light. Staring at them, I began to realise that they were not yet set but were waiting on my partnership! They weren't a 'positively', but rather a possibility. Isn't that just mind-blowing?

Activation

1. Find a space to be with Holy Spirit and invite Him to show you your book that is being written in heaven. You might go somewhere, like I did, or you might find a book simply be shown to you where you are; you might even have an angel come visit and show it to you! There are no limits or prescriptions to how we encounter and receive revelation from heaven.

2. Have a look at the front cover. What does it look like? What colour is it? What is the title of your book? What is the writing like? Remember to look at the details and ask questions.

3. Capture the first thought that goes through your mind and go with that, as long as it is encouraging, strengthening, and comforting.

4. Keep asking God questions about the book. What does the title mean? Is there a picture or colour that is on the front cover?

5. Ask Holy Spirit to show you some pages. What do you see on the pages there?

6. Write down/draw what you get and then spend some time thanking Jesus for your book and what Holy Spirit has shown you.

Groups

1. Leader: play some soaking music in the background to set the atmosphere.

2. Lead people in the activation steps above.

3. Be sure to have them write down/ draw what they see/feel/sense/hear.

4. Have everyone share what they saw about their books.

5. After each person shares, have the leader and others in the group call out some affirmations around what was shared and/or any prophetic words for the person that confirms and/or adds to what they shared. This should be a really encouraging experience where each person is validated and celebrated.

6. Pray for each person after they share. Have everyone reach out or gather round to participate in praying. If the group is very large, do this in smaller groups of around 6-8 people in each.

4. Sacred Space

Activation

1. Go to your secret place, the place you love to go to meet with Jesus where you can be undistracted. Turn your affections to Him.

2. "Come up here …" (Revelation 4:1) is your invitation today! Ask Him to take you and show you a 'heavenly room/space/place'. (You may begin to feel/see/sense/smell/become aware of the area around you, or the area in your imagination space. All are valid. Lean in).

3. Take note of where Holy Spirit has taken you. Look at the details. What do you see there?

4. Where is Jesus in the space? How do you feel?

5. Is there something He wants to tell you or give you in this space/place? Take it and take note of what it is. Look at the details again and ask Him questions. Asking questions is what will give you a more detailed experience and word.

6. Linger there, explore, and enjoy!

7. Write down/draw what you have seen, encountered, and received in this activation.

Groups

1. Leaders: Have everyone find their own space where they can get comfortable and be able to tune into Holy Spirit.

2. You might want to play some soaking music softly in the background.

3. Now lead the group through the above activation. Be sure to pace it so that people have time to encounter with some depth.

4. Leave space for them to write down/draw what they get/see in the activation.

5. Ask the group some leading questions about where their space was. Don't have them share anything just yet, just their space. For example, ask: 'Who found themselves in a room? Who found themselves in an outdoor place? Who was near water, e.g., river, sea, or waterfall? Who was in a forest or garden?

6. As people put up their hands, have all those with the same or similar, gather in one group. For example, all those who found themselves in a room, become one group; all those who were by water, become another group, etc.

7. If there is someone who has a unique situation and found themselves somewhere no-one else was, have them share what it was with the whole group. It's good to hear the 'out of the box' encounters as these stretch us! Then have them choose what is closest to their encounter or what group they would like to join.

8. In their small groups, have everyone share their encounter and compare what they saw and experienced.

9. Come back as a whole group and have a few people share.

Faith in our ability to encounter the realm of the spirit and of heaven is built when we realise others have had similar experiences.

5. News Flash

Every day we are reading or hearing different headlines about what is happening in our world. Most of it is pretty negative and fear based.

I felt the invitation of Holy Spirit to come up higher. To come and sit with the Father and listen to *His* newsflash instead. Today we get to be heavenly reporters! What is He seeing? What is He decreeing? What is He declaring over your life; over your city; over your nation or over the nations? What is heaven seeing that isn't released …yet?!

1 Corinthians 2:10 says that Holy Spirit searches the deep things of God and reveals them to us!

Access supplied! Be expectant that you are going to see/hear/feel/know what is in the heart of the Father and then partner to release 'on earth as it is in heaven'.

Activation

1. Find a quiet spot or space to be alone with the Father. Matthew 6:6 says He is in the secret place – go there!

2. Lean in. Invite Holy Spirit to awaken your senses to His Presence and to the realm of the Spirit. You can put your hands over your eyes, ears and heart and pray this simple prayer: "Eyes – be opened to the realm of the spirit; Ears – be opened to hear the voice of the Lord; Heart – be receptive to receive and perceive all that Holy Spirit wants to reveal to me. In Jesus Name, Amen."

3. What is the 'Newsflash or Headline' that He wants you to report on and declare? It could be over your life (personally), or it could be over your city, nation or even the nations! (* It doesn't have to be for all of the categories suggested, just pick one. And it doesn't have to be long. Just a headline.)

4. Write it down and then declare it.

Groups

Materials: old newspapers and magazines; poster paper; glue; scissors; colours/pencils.

1. Leaders: Have everyone find their own space where they can get comfortable and be able to tune into Holy Spirit.

2. Lead the group through the above activation. Be sure to pace it so that they have time to encounter and write down/draw what they get.

3. Now have everyone get up and create their 'Newsflash' using the newspapers and old magazines. You can use pictures or words, or both. Be creative!

4. Bring the group back together and have each come out to show and tell their 'Newsflash'.

5. Have one or two pray as everyone holds up their newsflashes to be released into the airwaves.

CHAPTER 9

Positioned in the Word

*"For the word of God is alive and powerful.
It is sharper than the sharpest two-edged sword…"*
Hebrews 4:12 (NLT)

Do you see that?

The Word of God is alive and powerful. It is timeless. It is life changing. It is a lamp and a light, showing us the way. Some have paid with their very lives for it.

It is still the world's number one top selling book. That is just mind-blowing! It doesn't make sense in the natural, however this is no ordinary book. It is supernaturally inspired and orchestrated by God Himself.

And that is the key! This book was breathed on by Holy Spirit and continues to be breathed on by Holy Spirit!

When we read the Bible, we should have an expectation that we are going to experience more. More of Jesus and more of the realm of the Spirit.

I love the saying, 'The Word (Bible) should lead to the Word (Jesus).'

When I read the Bible, I am blown away by how normal it was for every believer to encounter and experience God and the realm of the spirit – not just internally but in every way.

What we call radical is often just Biblically normal!

When we come to the Bible, our goal should never just be about getting 'information' but rather for encounter and transformation. The words in this book are supernatural. I know I said it before, but I'll say it again, they were inspired by Holy Spirit Himself!

The Bible is one of the only books you'll probably ever get to read with the author sitting right there with you!

When we position ourselves in the Word of God, we are positioning ourselves for spiritual and supernatural encounters.

The Word becomes the banks to the river of God flowing in and through us.

The written (logos) and spoken (rhema) Words of God are like a plug being put into the power socket in the wall. Put together, suddenly the current of heaven has a connection point and a place to flow in great power.

Have you ever seen a fire-breather? Someone who performs by putting fuel in their mouth and then lighting it? They are incredibly entertaining, and it looks thrilling and dangerous all at the same time!

Imagine the paraffin that fire-breathers use, is the written Word (the Logos). Just as the fire-breather puts it into his mouth, so too do we with the written Word. We love it, read it, digest it, meditate on it, and memorise it. It's in our heart and on our lips. Now, imagine that the spoken Words of God (the Rhema) through Holy Spirit, is the flame. When that flame of the spoken Word hits the fuel of the written Word, the result is an incredible release of fire!

There is so much that Holy Spirit wants to say to us; so much He wants to reveal to us; and so many ways He wants to encounter us through the very written words in our Bibles.

As you read your Bible, why don't you lean over to the author, Holy Spirit, and ask Him to reveal something new to you or take you into a fresh encounter of His Presence?

You won't regret it!

ACTIVATE

1. Throne Room Encounter

One amazing way to practise 'seeing' and activating the seer gift is to invite Holy Spirit to take you into a Biblical encounter.

What do I mean by this?

Let me first start by telling you what I don't mean! I am not saying that we are going to change Scripture in any way, and I am not saying we are going to add to Scripture.

I am saying that there is an invitation to the 'more' that Scripture has, and Holy Spirit is the One to ask. There are depths in the Word to be mined and experienced. Treasures to be found!

Holy Spirit can reveal Scripture to us in this way because He is God. He wrote it and He stands outside of time itself. He is the Spirit of Revelation.

This is another way He trains us to SEE. It activates and opens up the eyes of our heart.

The 'Word' (Logos or written Word) should always lead us to the WORD (Rhema or Jesus Himself, the Living Word).

Activation

You will need your Bible, a piece of paper or journal and pen/colours.

1. Invite Holy Spirit, the Spirit of Truth and Revelation, to come right now, right where you are.
2. Open the Bible to the book of Revelation 4:1-3 (NLT).
3. Read Verse 1: "Then as I looked, I saw a door standing open in heaven …" (Pause)

   - I want you to see this. Picture what this heavenly door looks like.
   - Ask Holy Spirit to show you/reveal details to you.
   - Draw/write down what you see.

4. "… and the same voice I had heard before spoke to me like a trumpet blast." (Pause)

   - Can you hear this voice or sound? Do you sense what it is like? How does it make you feel? Take a moment to ask Holy Spirit to open up your senses to it and become aware of the 'sound'.
   - Draw/write what you 'hear' or sense.

5. Verse 2: "And instantly I was in the Spirit ..." (Pause)

    - What does this FEEL like? And look like?
    - Pause again and tune in to your 'feelings'. Is it warm; is it electric; is it like running water or a cool breeze; is it like fire?
    - Take a moment and write down what you feel.

6. "... and I saw a throne in heaven and someone sitting on it." (Pause)

    - What does the throne look like?
    - Can you see the One sitting on it?
    - What does He look like?
    - Write/draw what you see.

7. Verse 3: "The one sitting on the throne was as brilliant as gemstones—like jasper and carnelian. And the glow of an emerald circled his throne like a rainbow."

    - How do you feel right now being in this space?
    - Is the One on the throne aware of you? Is He looking at you?
    - What do you think He wants to tell you?
    - You might feel it/hear it with your ears or mind or know it.
    - Write/draw what you feel/sense.

8. Take a deep breath and thank the Lord for His incredible, living Word and the encounter you have just had!

Groups

1. Play some soaking music softly in the background.
2. Have everyone find a space where they can focus on and connect individually to the Presence of God.
3. Make sure everyone has their journal and a pen/colour pencils with them.

4. Leader: read through the above activation. Be sure to pace it so that people really can meditate on it and experience what you are leading them through.

5. Have people answer the questions in their journal, either writing them down or drawing what they see.

6. When you finish, have people come up to share their experiences.

2. Rest for your Soul

> *"The Lord is my best friend and my shepherd.*
> *I always have more than enough.*
> *He offers a resting place for me in his luxurious love"*
> *Psalm 23:1-2 (TPT)*

What a beautiful and timely reminder considering what is going on in the world right now!

I sense Holy Spirit whisper an invitation: "Let me refresh your soul (your mind, will and emotions) today."

Activation

1. Find a quiet spot, where you can be alone with Jesus.

2. Invite Holy Spirit to come and fill your whole being. Take a deep breath. Breathe in His Presence.

3. Then breathe out – release all anxiety, fear, worry, pressure, busyness, distraction…and anything else that comes to mind.

4. Read Psalm 23 out loud. It's important to speak it as well as hear it.

> "The Lord is my shepherd.
> I have all that I need.
> He lets me rest in green meadows,
> he leads me beside peaceful streams.

> He renews my strength.
> He guides me along right paths,
> bringing honour to his name.
> Even when I walk
> through the darkest valley,
> I will not be afraid,
> for you are close beside me.
> Your rod and your staff
> protect and comfort me.
> You prepare a feast for me
> in the presence of my enemies.
> You honour me by anointing my head with oil.
> My cup overflows with blessings.
> Surely your goodness and unfailing love will pursue me
> all the days of my life,
> and I will live in the house of the Lord forever."
> Psalm 23 (NLT)

5. Ask Holy Spirit to take you to your 'resting place'. David's 'resting place' in this Psalm was green meadows. Yours may be different. (It could be anywhere! For example, the beach, a river, the top of a mountain, in a field of flowers … these are just examples.) There is no formula or limit to where He wants to take you today. It will be unique and personal, and Jesus is waiting there for you.

6. You might get a picture/feeling/word/knowing about where you have just been taken.
Some of you will even feel as though you have been literally taken there. Lean into what is happening and trust Holy Spirit.

7. Where are you? What is your surrounding? Can you feel or smell anything? What are the colours or sounds that you see and hear? Linger here.

8. Where is Jesus? What does He look like? Spend time with Him in His luxurious love. What does that look like or feel like?

9. What does He want to say/impart to you? Maybe it's just a time to rest with Him? How do you feel in this place. Remember that the reason He is bringing you here is to refresh and restore your soul (your mind, will and emotions).

10. Give Jesus anything that has robbed you of 'rest' in your soul. It might be pain; it might be fear; it might be weariness; it might be disappointment…This is the 'valley of the shadow of death'.

11. Declare out loud, right now: 'I will not be afraid because Jesus is with me.'

12. Now breathe. Take a deep breath and breathe in His Presence. It is fresh and healing! Breathe out all the 'stuff' that hinders love and depletes your energy and joy. Repeat. Breathe Him in; breathe the rest out.

13. Now see Him pour out oil over your head. What does that feel like or look like? Does it have a scent? He is anointing you afresh.

14. Ask Him, "What are you anointing me for?"

15. Be sure to thank Him for such a sweet time and write down or draw your experience with him.

16. If you want to take it further, use the full chapter to experience more! You might want to look at the blessings that are talked about in the Psalm, and what they are specifically. Ask Jesus.

17. What does that look like to have goodness and mercy follow you?

Go as deep and as long as you want to.

Selah.

Groups

1. Play some soaking music softly in the background.

2. Have everyone find a space where they can focus on and connect individually to the Presence of God.

3. Make sure everyone has their journal and a pen/colour pencils with them.
4. Leader: read through Psalm 23 out loud. You may also want to put it up on a screen.
5. Now the leader reads through the above activation. Be sure to pace it so that people really can meditate and experience what you are leading them through.
6. Give the group time to write down and/or draw what they see and/or experience.
7. Once time is up, have one or two share with the whole group.
8. Get the rest to turn to a partner and share their experiences with each other and bless one another.

3. House of God, the Gate of Heaven – You're it!

> *"As he slept, he dreamed of a stairway that reached from the earth up to heaven. And he saw the angels of God going up and down the stairway."*
> Genesis 28:12 (NLT)

> *"But he was also afraid and said, "What an awesome place this is! It is none other than the house of God, the very gateway to heaven!"*
> Genesis 28:17 (NLT)

The *'house of God'* that Jacob saw in this encounter was marked by supernatural activity. Angels ascending and descending. There was no literal house or structure there. So, then what did he see?

In John 1:51, we see angels ascending and descending on a person – Jesus! He became the very access point between heaven and earth.

Jesus, the Son of God, made it possible for us humans to be forgiven, come into right relationship with God, be *filled* with the Spirit and as a result, become 'houses of God'.

That is your inheritance!

Could it be that angels are still ascending and descending on Jesus' followers today? We get to be living, breathing, moving houses of God that become the very gateway for not only heaven to be released here on earth but for others to enter into and encounter heaven!

Activation

1. Get into your secret place. Read Genesis 28:10-17 & John 1:51. Picture what that may look like.
2. Now invite Holy Spirit to reveal to you the angels that are ascending and descending over you, or in your room, right now. (You might see/feel/hear/sense something.)
3. What does that look like? What are the angels like? How do you feel? Look at the details and ask more questions.
4. Now ask Holy Spirit:
    - What is something specific that is being released to me from heaven right now?
    - What is something you want me to release 'to heaven' from me right now?
    - What is something that is being released from heaven for me to GIVE AWAY and who is it for?
5. Be sure to write down and/or draw your experience.
6. Write down a prophetic 'letter' to the person that Holy Spirit revealed to you, giving them what was released from heaven and why.
7. Message that person with your prophetic 'letter' or, alternatively, voice record the letter and then send it to that person to bless their day!

Groups

Materials: Paper and pens/colours/markers. Hand out 2 pieces of paper to everyone in the group.

1. Play some soaking music quietly in the background.
2. Have everyone find a space in the room.
3. Read Genesis 28:10-17 and John 1:51 to the group.
4. Pray and invite Holy Spirit to reveal angels ascending and descending over each person or in the room. Give them time to tune in and see/sense/feel/perceive the angelic activity. It may not be clear but don't discount the small 'sense' or knowing that you might have.
5. Ask them to look at the details and ask these questions:
   - What does it look like to see angels ascending and descending?
   - What are the angels like?
   - How do you feel right now in this atmosphere? Look at the details and ask more questions.
   - Is there a doorway? Is there a ladder? Is there a colour or cloud?
6. Now ask Holy Spirit:
   - What is something specific that is being released to me from heaven right now?
   - What is something you want me to release 'to heaven' from me right now?
   - What is something that is being released from heaven for me to GIVE AWAY to someone else.
7. Be sure to pace this part so that people have time to write down and/or draw their answers on their piece of paper.
8. Now spend time writing down a prophetic 'letter' with what Holy Spirit released for you to give away from heaven. You don't need to address it or know who it is for.
9. Have the group pair up randomly and then read the letter they wrote to each other and give it to them as a prophetic gift.
10. Be sure to pray for each other after you have done that and bless one another.

4. Strengthen Yourself in the Lord

"...But David strengthened himself in the Lord His God."
1 Samuel 30:6 (ESV)

"Seek more of his strength! Seek more of him!
Let's always be seeking the light of his face."
Psalm 105:4 (TPT)

In a time where everything around us is clamouring for our attention, distracting us, and literally draining our very souls, let's be those who run to the Word and find strength in the Lord our God just like David did.

Activation

1. Find a space to be with Jesus where you won't be distracted. You might want to play some soaking worship music softly in the background.
2. Now let your heart's affection focus on Jesus and begin to be stirred in love for Him. Invite Holy Spirit to help you to become fully aware of Jesus. Look for the light of His face.
3. Now ask Holy Spirit to show you an area of your life He would love to strengthen. It might be in your physical health; it might be your mind or mental health; it might be your heart or emotional health. Remember, you might hear/feel/sense/see or simply know. All are valid.
4. First, give Jesus your weakness. You might want to see where Jesus is in relation to you. Is He in front of you or next to you or behind you or above you? See Him. He is love and He is safe.
5. Now ask Jesus: What do you want to give me that will release strength?
6. Take it! He might want you to put something on. Or He may lay His hands on you to release healing or impartation. Maybe He wants to infuse you with His strength. He may give you something to eat. Wait a moment to see and receive.

7. Now, ask Holy Spirit to highlight a Bible verse or person from the Bible in relation to what He has been doing in you.

8. Look up what He shows you in the Bible and spend time with Holy Spirit, asking Him how to apply what He is showing you. The goal is transformation by the Word (Logos and Rhema together).

9. Ask Holy Spirit to show, tell or give you a scripture, promise or a prophetic declaration you can apply to your life to strengthen you. This is going to be something you can take daily like vitamins or something you can fight with, like Paul told Timothy (1 Timothy 1:18), or even something you can put up as a powerful declaration of hope. The Word really is alive, but we need to apply it by faith.

10. Be sure to write/draw all that you have experienced.

11. Take time to thank Jesus for the way He has strengthened you.

Groups

Put up the scriptures: 1 Samuel 30:6 NKJV & Psalm 105:4 TPT

1. Play some soaking music quietly in the background.

2. Have everyone find a space in the room. Be sure to have your journals or paper with you.

3. Leader: Take everyone through the above activation. Be sure to pace it so that people can engage with what Holy Spirit is revealing.

4. When everyone has written down their Scripture, promise or prophetic declaration have them find a partner in the room.

5. When everyone has a partner, have them release the Scripture, promise or prophetic declaration over their partner and pray for an impartation of supernatural strength in the Lord over one another.

5. Psalm 25 and a Path

For the majority of 2020 and 2021 we were in Stage 4 Lockdown which meant we could not leave our homes and if we did, it was only for essentials and walking (within 5kms). We were told we could walk with one other person. These walks became so integral to keeping our souls healthy. I came to love those times! Today there is an invitation from our best Friend, King Jesus, to come walk with Him. There is something special about being outside, especially with friends or those we love.

Jesus is calling you to have a walk and a 'heart-to-heart' with Him today. Will you respond?

Activation

1. Welcome Holy Spirit! Take a moment to make some intentional space for Him to come. Let yourself lean into His Presence. Leaning in is simply coming close – like leaning in for a whisper. Tune into Him and ask Him to awaken your senses again.
2. For this activation, you are going to take a walk with Jesus on a path. It can be a virtual-reality Holy Spirit inspired walk or a literal walk.
3. First, be sure to read and meditate on Psalm 25:4-5 & 8-10.
4. Now it's time to take that walk! As you begin to walk, take note of where Jesus is. Is He beside you, behind you or in front of you? Ask Him why.
5. Consider a decision you need to make or a problem that you might be facing (or a loved one is facing). It can be big or small. With that in mind, imagine yourself taking Jesus' hand and walking hand-in-hand with him.
6. Ask Him what path you are to take as you are navigating through this decision or problem.
7. Let David's words in Psalm 16 inspire you: "I have set the Lord before me. Because he is at my right hand, I will not be shaken. Therefore, my heart is glad, and my tongue rejoices; my body will also rest secure…

> You have made known to me the path of life; you will fill me with joy in your presence, with eternal pleasures at your right hand." (verses 8-11 NIV)

8. What is Jesus saying to you on your path? What is He releasing or speaking over you and your situation right now?

9. Now ask Him to release joy to you. In His Presence there is always fullness of joy, and the joy of the Lord is your strength. (Nehemiah 8:10)

10. Write down and/or draw all about your walk with Jesus.

Groups

Put up the Scriptures: Psalm 25:4-5 & 8-10

1. Play some soaking music quietly in the background.

2. Have everyone find a space in the room. Be sure to have your journals or paper with you.

3. Leader: Take everyone through the above activation. Be sure to pace it so that people are able to engage with it.

4. Have the group come back together and invite a few to come up and share their experiences.

5. Leader: Now have everyone posture themselves to receive. Tell them, "Get ready!" And release joy over everyone. Allow Holy Spirit to come and bring His supernatural, healing, strengthening joy! Don't rush this part – be sure to allow Holy Spirit to move and people to receive. This is going to be powerful!

CHAPTER 10

Positioned for Impact

It was early 2020 and the world had suddenly been thrust into a media-driven pandemic of seemingly apocalyptic proportions. Food and toilet paper (you all remember *that* don't you?!) were being stripped from the shops as people began panic buying, stocking up for the unknown.

One particular day, I had to run up to the local shops for some essential items, as we too were running low, before everything went into lockdown. As I stepped into the shops, the atmosphere of panic, fear and hopelessness engulfed me, and it was so overwhelming that I literally began to sob and had to put my hand over my mouth to stifle it. I had to get out of there. I quickly bought what I needed and went home as fast as possible. As soon as I walked through my front door, I felt a wave of peace. Phew! However, as I was feeling relieved to be in my 'safe place', Holy Spirit began to speak to me very clearly. He gently but firmly asked me this question: "you know that I've made you to *feel* atmospheres so that you can *shift* them … don't you?" All of a sudden, it was like a light-bulb moment. The reason I became aware of the extreme hopelessness all around me was so that I could release hope from heaven's realm!

I purposefully went back out and began to walk up and down the shops, quietly praying in my heavenly language and singing under my breath: "Jesus, Jesus, You make the darkness tremble". As I released hope into the atmosphere, I intentionally began making eye contact with people – connecting with them, smiling, and asking how they were going.

I went into a charcoal chicken shop where the news of global uncertainty was blaring from the TV. Everyone seemed mesmerised by fear. The owner of the shop was staring in disbelief and despair at what was happening. I went up to him and asked him how he was feeling and, as he opened up, I was able to take his hand and share hope in Jesus Name and pray for him and his business. His wife came out and ran over to me and gave me a massive hug!

Releasing the Kingdom looks like something!
It looks like Jesus stepping in.

Proximity to Jesus positions us to become acutely alert and aware of the reality of the realm of the spirit and of heaven, and then we get to do what we have been called to do.

This goes for us as individuals and as the church.

We are heavenly releasers.
We are light bearers.
We are agents of hope.
We are channels of love.
We are Kingdom activators.
We are divine solutionaries.

This is who we are, and this is our mission – to release on earth as it is in heaven.

ACTIVATE

1. Keys!

As I spent time with Holy Spirit, I heard the words *"keys, keys and strategies"*.

I love old keys! They can be ornate and beautiful, and they also carry significance in the prophetic. Keys speak about access and Kingdom authority.

> *"And I will give you the keys of the Kingdom of Heaven.*
> *Whatever you forbid on earth will be forbidden*
> *in heaven, and whatever you permit on earth*
> *will be permitted in heaven."*
> *Matthew 16:19 (NLT)*

Activation

1. Look for a key in your home that you don't use very often. It can be an actual key (old or new/big or small) or an ornamental key.

2. Spend time with Holy Spirit and ask Him to speak to you about that key. We are looking at the 'natural' as a catalyst to hear/see what Holy Spirit is wanting to say in the spiritual.

   - What is on His heart in relation to the key and what it opens.
   - Write/draw what you hear/see.

3. Ask Him to enlarge your vision and see what He has to say about your next step and an opening that He has for you.

   - It may be a door of opportunity.
   - It may be a new level of Kingdom Authority to walk in.
   - It may be access to something you haven't had access to before.

4. Write down or draw what you see and experience.

5. Take time to thank Jesus for this key and if there is anything He wants you to do or put in place with what He has shown you.

Groups

Part 1: Personal

Leader: Put up a prophetic picture of an old key or keys. Alternatively, you may wish to bring in an old key as a prop to show.

Help set the atmosphere by playing some prophetic, instrumental music softly in the background.

1. Leader: read through these steps with the group.

2. Jesus is going to give you a KEY. As you quiet your mind down and lean into His Presence, see Him before you.

> He is giving you a KEY. You might have a picture in your mind; a thought; a knowing; a feeling.
>
> 3. Take the Key. What does it look like? Is there anything written on it or is there a design inscribed on it?
> 4. Ask Him: "What is this Key for?" Can you see a door that this Key is to unlock? Is there something written on the door? (e.g., Breakthrough or Healing)
> Be sure to allow time for people to write down what they see/hear.
> 5. Invite someone up to share what they got.
> 6. Is there anyone in the room that needs that? (e.g., healing/freedom/breakthrough)
> 7. Ask that person who received the key to release that 'key' over those that responded.

Part 2: Nation

> 1. Now we are going to ask Holy Spirit to reveal a 'KEY' for our nation.
> 2. Take time to connect in again with Holy Spirit.
> 3. Ask Him: "What is on your heart to unlock and release in, over and through our nation?"
> 4. Look at the details. Remember, ask Holy Spirit questions.
> 5. Have people step up and share what they saw/got and then pray declaration prayers in line with what they were given.

2. God's Heavenly Solutionaries!

Did you know, friend of God, that you are called to be a mountain-mover, giant-slayer, heaven-releaser? Your friendship and partnership with Father, Son, and Holy Spirit positions you to shift atmospheres and release heaven's solutions for earth's impossibilities!

In Isaiah 1:18, God invites Isaiah to "come and let us reason together …"

What I saw in the Spirit realm was a heavenly boardroom with a big resource cupboard at the back. I saw the Father at the table in this boardroom – much like a CEO of a company!

The Father is inviting you to come to Him today for heavenly solutions.

Activation

1. Find a place/space to sit with the Father. Remember Matthew 6:6 tells you where He's waiting!

2. Invite Holy Spirit into that space with you to reveal the Father and what is in the depths of His heart. (1 Corinthians 2:10)

3. What impossibility do you see around you (it could be personal, corporate, governmental, national, international, etc.)?
It may be the most blatantly obvious thing (like a war or a current global or national crisis) or it may be something hidden or less obvious, or very personal. Be sure to ask Holy Spirit because the Father may have something else to talk to you about.

4. Bring that problem to the 'table' and then ask Him these questions:

    - "Father, what do you want to declare over this?"
    - "Father, what solution do you have and want me to release?"
    - "Father, what do you want to 'give' me from the resources of heaven for this?"
    - "Father, show me if there is something practical I can do?"

5. Be sure to write down everything He tells you.

6. Spend some time thanking Him for sharing His heart with you and entrusting you with it.

7. Pray and partner with what was shared with you, to release 'on earth as it is in heaven' right now.

Groups

Leader: Hand out a piece of A4 paper to everyone in the group.

1. Play some soaking music quietly in the background.
2. Have everyone find a space in the room. Be sure they have their journals and paper with them.
3. Leader: Take everyone through the above activation. Be sure to pace it so that people are able to engage with it.
4. When it comes to the impossibilities, have everyone write those on their piece of A4 paper.
5. Have everyone write the answers to the questions from the Father above (in Step 4) in their journals.
6. Once they have had time to answer all the questions, have everyone put their A4 piece of paper on the ground and stand on them.
7. Now have everyone begin to partner with what the Father showed them or told them and read their answers out loud over their situations. It will be all at once and messy, but this is ok!
8. Re-group and take time to thank and praise the Father for all that has been released over every impossibility.

3. Cry out for the Nations – Go to the Nations

"Ask of Me and I will give You the nations for your inheritance ..."
Psalm 2:8 (NKJV)

In my worship time, Holy Spirit had me lay across a world map and I began to cry out for the nations. As I wept over the nations, I began to think about a specific nation that had come to mind and then pictured myself there in that nation, on the ground. What happened next was an incredible encounter where I got to walk the streets with Jesus, love on people in that nation, release hope and blow the breath of life in the atmosphere. I got to hug people who were lonely, sick, isolated, and afraid. We visited a hospital where I prayed for the sick and spoke hope to the doctors and nurses!

I love that we are not limited and restricted when it comes to the realm of the Spirit.

So today you're invited to do the same. No border is closed, and no-where is off limits!

Activation

1. Go to your secret place and put on some worship music.
2. If you have a world map, get it out or look one up on your mobile/iPad.
3. Begin to worship and release a song over the nations. Spend some time releasing the sound of worship.
4. Now ask Holy Spirit to highlight a nation to you (you may already have one on your heart).
   Using your imagination, picture that place. If you've been there before, see yourself there. If you've never been before, think about a famous landmark that you can picture in your mind's eye (e.g., the Eiffel Tower; the Taj Mahal, etc.).
5. Ask Holy Spirit to take you there. For some it will be more like looking at a picture and for others, you are going to feel like you are on the ground there. Both are valid. Steward whatever it is He is showing you.
   Become aware of the surroundings. If there are people, look at them; look them in the eyes; be moved with compassion. What do you see? What do you feel?
6. What does Holy Spirit want you to do? You may feel to do a dance that releases captives; you may touch people or the land itself, and release healing; you might see yourself in a hospital speaking hope and courage to those there, you may even see yourself with government officials or in a lab with scientists looking for a scientific breakthrough.

Remember, there are NO LIMITATIONS and NO RESTRICTIONS in the realm of the spirit!

Partner with all that Holy Spirit shows or tells you.

7. Take time to finish up by blessing that nation and thanking Holy Spirit for letting you partner with Him in the nations, from the comfort of your own home!

8. Listen out in the coming days for news about the nation you have prayed for. Expect a supernatural shift to have happened as you released on earth as it is in heaven.

Groups

1. Leader: Put up a world map and/or have some printed out with the names of pre-selected nations.

2. Put everyone into groups of 3-5.

3. Give 1 print-out to each group with the name of a nation on it.

4. Leader: take the whole group through this activation by reading out the steps below. Be sure to pace it so that everyone has time to engage and participate.

5. Using your imagination, picture that place. If you've been there before, see yourself there. If you've never been, think about a famous landmark that you can picture in your mind's eye (e.g., the Eiffel Tower; the Taj Mahal, etc.).

6. Ask Holy Spirit to take you there. For some it will be more like looking at a picture and for others, you are going to feel like you are on the ground there. Both are valid. Steward whatever it is He is showing you.
Become aware of the surroundings. If there are people, look at them; look them in the eyes; be moved with compassion. What do you see? What do you feel?

7. What does Holy Spirit want you to do? You may feel to do a dance that releases captives; you may touch people or the land itself, and release healing; you might see yourself in a hospital speaking hope and courage to those there, you may even see yourself with government officials or in a lab with scientists looking for a scientific breakthrough.

> **Remember, there's NO LIMITATIONS and NO RESTRICTIONS in the realm of the spirit!**
>
> 8. When time is up, have everyone share within their group what Holy Spirit showed and told them during the activation.
> 9. Are there any similarities with those in your group?
> 10. Pray for the nation in your small group.
> 11. Come back together as a whole group and worship together over the nations.

4. Declarations for Nations

Activation

> *"Declaring the things that are not as though they were…"*
> Romans 4:17

This activation is about looking beyond yourself. This is about your Nation. We are going to tune into Presence and hear/sense/discern/see the heart and the 'words of God' for where we live.

*Our prophetic declarations are as powerful
in our mouths as they are in God's.*

> 1. Posture yourself in a place where you can tune into Holy Spirit. Invite His Presence to come and fill you. Breathe Him in deeply. Let your love for Jesus well up within you and stay in that place for a while.
> 2. What is the 'now' word that the Father is speaking over your Nation? It could be where you currently live or the nation you, or your family, have come from originally.
> 3. Ask Holy Spirit to speak one or two key/strategic words that are on the heart of the Father for your Nation.

> 4. Out of that 'word' create a prophetic declaration for your Nation. Remember to call out the 'gold'!

This is my (Gabby's) example for my own beloved nation, Australia, where I live:

So, my words that I got were, *Revival Glory*.

"I declare that Australia is indeed the Great South Land of the Holy Spirit. That now is the time for Revival Glory! She is being called to step into an epoch of Glory. These will be known as her Glory days. The Lord says, 'I am unstopping the wells of revival once again.' It will be as the gold rush days. People will come from everywhere to find 'gold' in Australia – the gold of His Presence!"

Groups

1. Play some instrumental worship music softly in the background.
2. Ask everyone to find a space on their own.
3. Leader: Read through the above activation to the group, making sure to pace it so that everyone can engage and encounter.
4. Ask Holy Spirit to speak one or two key/strategic words that are on the heart of the Father for your Nation. This could be where you currently live or where you or your family come from originally.
5. Out of that 'word' create a prophetic declaration for your Nation. Remember to call out the 'gold'!
6. Write those down in your journal or on a piece of paper.
7. Leader: Have everyone get into groups of 4.
8. Each person shares their prophetic declaration for their nation.
9. Then partner with each other's prophetic declarations and come into agreement to see "His Kingdom come, and His will be done right here, right now, as it is in heaven!"

5. Releasing Heaven's Joy

"For the Kingdom of God… is righteousness, peace and joy in the Holy Spirit."
Romans 14:17 (NIV)

Did you know that joy is a third of the Kingdom? When we release 'on earth as it is in heaven', JOY is part of what we get to see manifested in and around us!

Joy is a Person and His name is Jesus.

Activation

Materials: 2 pieces of A4 paper; pen/markers; phone to record.

1. Go to your secret place and invite Holy Spirit to come and reveal Himself to you there.
2. On your piece of paper, write down the things that you are struggling with, contending for, wrestling with, believing for breakthroughs; holding onto; etc. (It might be one thing or many different things but keep them as dot points).
3. When you've written everything on your paper, put it down on the floor in front of you.
4. On your second piece of A4 paper, in BIG letters, write the word JOY (you may want to use colours).
5. Put your JOY paper on top of the first page that is on the floor.
6. As an act of 'faith', step onto the JOY and begin to release joy over every situation you have written down on your first paper. You might want to dance on it; you might want to praise or worship as you stand on it; you might want to laugh over it or even blow bubbles over it!

It is important that you DO SOMETHING! Your breakthrough is coming through the release of JOY, but you have to step into it and partner with heaven to see it released.

7. Record what Holy Spirit says to you in this activation on your phone (download a voice app if you don't have one already). Prophetic recordings can become our marker moments and memorial stones!

Groups

Give out paper and pens/textas/markers to everyone in the group.
Give out bubbles.
Make sure they have their phones ready to record the prophetic declaration of joy at the end.

1. Leader: Take your group through the activation steps above.
2. When you get to step 5, have everyone hold up their paper with the word JOY on it.
3. Ask everyone to find a partner.
4. Leader: Continue to read through step 6 and have everyone step onto their pieces of paper.
5. Everyone now takes a moment to listen to Holy Spirit for a prophetic faith 'act' that they are going to tell their partner to do. For example, they might say to "jump up and down on your paper"; or "laugh over your paper", etc.
It is important that everyone DOES SOMETHING!
Explain to the group their breakthrough is coming through the release of JOY, but they have to step into it and partner with heaven to see it released.
6. Then blow bubbles over one another and partner with Joy! Have each person take some time to pray for their partner, as they blow their bubbles, and release a prophetic word to encourage and exhort them. Be sure to use your phones to record the prophetic words given.

ACTIVATE BONUS

Christmas Activation: The Christmas Gift

Once upon a time some wise men followed a star and brought gifts of Gold, Frankincense and Myrrh and laid them before a baby in a manger. They knew that this baby was the most significant baby to ever be born on earth. This baby would become the King of all Kings!

In 2 Samuel 24:24 (BSB), King David said, "I will not offer to the LORD my God burnt offerings that cost me nothing." Wow! Can we say the same?

So often we come to Jesus looking for something from Him rather than just being with Him. When is the last time you have given a gift to Jesus?

As I sat with the Lord, I began to feel the stir of Holy Spirit asking me to 'gift' Jesus with something of my choice. It was not easy! What do you bring to the King of Kings? My whole life, well – that's a given. But if Jesus was to stand before me right now, what is in my hands or my heart that would bless Him?

Activation

1. Find a quiet spot and turn your affection to Jesus. Ask Holy Spirit to come.
2. Jesus is standing right in front of you. Look at His face and His eyes! What love!
3. It's your turn to give Jesus a gift! What gift would/could you give Him?
4. What is valuable to you? What talent do you have? Maybe you would bring Him a song; maybe you would paint Him a picture? Maybe it's your job or your children? What is in your 'hand' or your 'heart' that is meaningful and you could lay down at the feet of Jesus?

> 5. What is Jesus' reaction to your gift? What does He say or do?
> 6. Write down Jesus' response to your gift as a personal letter. For example: Dear (insert your name here), Love from Jesus
> 7. Thank Him and spend some time together!

Groups

> 1. Play some instrumental worship music softly in the background.
> 2. Make sure everyone has their journals and a pen.
> 3. Leader: Lead the group through the above activation. Be sure to pace it so that people have time to encounter Jesus in the moment.
> 4. Now take time to have them write their letters from Jesus.
> 5. When the activation time is over, invite people to come up and share about their encounter and read out their letters.

Easter Activation: Good Friday – Resurrection Power

What a perfect time to stop and reflect with awe and wonder at the magnificent price that was paid for you and for me. It's a sombre and holy moment that we must never take for granted. Yet there is also excitement and anticipation because we know what's coming! King Jesus defeated death and rose again victoriously and triumphantly!

I felt Holy Spirit whisper to my heart: "Did you know that resurrection broke out when Jesus took His last breath?" Now, you know when Holy Spirit asks you a question it's not because He doesn't know the answer, don't you?

I had a look in the Bible, and this is what I found:

> *"Then Jesus shouted out again, and he released his spirit.*
> *At that moment the curtain in the sanctuary of the Temple*
> *was torn in two, from top to bottom.*

The earth shook, rocks split apart, and tombs opened. The bodies of many godly men and women who had died were raised from the dead."
Matthew 27:50-52 NLT

Do you see that? Jesus shouted out, released His Spirit and at THAT moment everything changed! The curtain was torn in two from top to bottom, the earth shook violently, and many tombs opened. Can you imagine it? And not only that, many who had died were raised from the dead. Resurrection power! That's our Jesus!

Activation

1. Go for a walk in your neighbourhood. Ask Holy Spirit to move you with His Love for the people around you.

2. As you walk, invite Holy Spirit to open your spiritual eyes and ears.

3. What does He want you to see and hear?

4. Begin by listening with your natural ears and looking with your natural eyes. What do you hear? What do you see? Listen to those sounds. Now ask Holy Spirit to speak to you through those.

5. Ask this question: "What is dead that needs resurrection Life right now?"

6. Begin declaring Life into the areas that Holy Spirit shows you. Call that which is dead to come alive! Release Resurrection Power!

Groups

Materials: A4 paper and pens/markers/sharpies.

1. For this activation, you may want to take your group outside the four walls of the house or building. If you can't, that is totally OK. You can still participate in the activation and partner with what Holy Spirit says or shows you.

2. If you are staying inside, encourage everyone to turn around and face towards the outside.

3. Leader: Take your group through the above activation steps. Whether it is a literal walk or not is entirely up to you.

4. Key question for the group is: "What is dead that needs resurrection Life right now?"

5. Have everyone write down/draw what they get.

6. Once they have had time to do that, get everyone to turn back in towards the inside and form a circle.

7. Have them hold up their paper for all to see and go around the group speaking out what needs resurrection Life.

8. As they speak that out, get them to lay their papers in the middle of the circle.

9. When everyone has shared, spend time praying together to declare and release resurrection Life over every situation.

Final Words

My hope and my heart is that this little book has not only been a blessing but a resource that has helped activate you and propel you into the adventure of living a life in the realm of the spirit. As you've journeyed through it, I pray that your spiritual senses have been awakened, heightened, and trained and that it has been a springboard to catapult you into realms of Presence.

The book is designed so you can pick it up and use it as many times as you like, in whatever order you like, so my encouragement is to do just that! Keep it somewhere close so that you can pull it out at any point and lead yourself or others into encounters with Him. I believe that each time, Holy Spirit will meet you and reveal something fresh and relevant to your 'now'. May it stir your heart evermore for the more!

If you leave this book having grown in your love for Father, Son, and Holy Spirit, more awakened to the realm of the spirit, stirred to partner with that realm and see 'on earth as it is in heaven', then my job is done.

"Holy Spirit, would you anoint every person that has read this book with the 'more'. That their spirit-senses would be awakened to you on a glorious, new level. May they have encounters after encounters that lead them to a life of passionate, fiery love. May they know Jesus more and more. I pray that what you have done *in* each of them, you will do *through* each of them. That this would just be the beginning! In Jesus' beautiful name. Amen."

www.ingramcontent.com/pod-product-compliance
Lightning Source LLC
Chambersburg PA
CBHW062049290426
44109CB00027B/2776